U.S. Economic Policy toward the Association of Southeast Asian Nations

LAWRENCE B. KRAUSE

U.S. Economic Policy toward the Association of Southeast Asian Nations

Meeting the Japanese Challenge

THE BROOKINGS INSTITUTION
Washington, D.C.

Copyright © 1982 by
THE BROOKINGS INSTITUTION
1775 Massachusetts Avenue, N.W., Washington, D.C. 20036

Library of Congress Cataloging in Publication data:

Krause, Lawrence B.
    U.S. economic policy toward the Association
of Southeast Asian Nations.
    Includes bibliographical references and
index.
    1. United States—Foreign economic relations
—Asia, Southeastern. 2. Asia, Southeastern—
Foreign economic relations—United States.
3. Japan—Foreign economic relations—Asia,
Southeastern. 4. Asia, Southeastern—Foreign
economic relations—Japan. 5. ASEAN.
I. Title.
HF1456.5.A7K72 1982   337.73059   82-9656
ISBN 0-8157-5026-9
ISBN 0-8157-5025-0 (pbk.)

1 2 3 4 5 6 7 8 9

THE BROOKINGS INSTITUTION is an independent organization devoted to nonpartisan research, education, and publication in economics, government, foreign policy, and the social sciences generally. Its principal purposes are to aid in the development of sound public policies and to promote public understanding of issues of national importance.

The Institution was founded on December 8, 1927, to merge the activities of the Institute for Government Research, founded in 1916, the Institute of Economics, founded in 1922, and the Robert Brookings Graduate School of Economics and Government, founded in 1924.

The Board of Trustees is responsible for the general administration of the Institution, while the immediate direction of the policies, program, and staff is vested in the President, assisted by an advisory committee of the officers and staff. The by-laws of the Institution state: "It is the function of the Trustees to make possible the conduct of scientific research, and publication, under the most favorable conditions, and to safeguard the independence of the research staff in the pursuit of their studies and in the publication of the results of such studies. It is not a part of their function to determine, control, or influence the conduct of particular investigations or the conclusions reached."

The President bears final responsibility for the decision to publish a manuscript as a Brookings book. In reaching his judgment on the competence, accuracy, and objectivity of each study, the President is advised by the director of the appropriate research program and weighs the views of a panel of expert outside readers who report to him in confidence on the quality of the work. Publication of a work signifies that it is deemed a competent treatment worthy of public consideration but does not imply endorsement of conclusions or recommendations.

The Institution maintains its position of neutrality on issues of public policy in order to safeguard the intellectual freedom of the staff. Hence interpretations or conclusions in Brookings publications should be understood to be solely those of the authors and should not be attributed to the Institution, to its trustees, officers, or other staff members, or to the organizations that support its research.

Foreword

Not too long ago Americans were hardly aware of the existence of the Association of Southeast Asian Nations (ASEAN). However, owing to the rapid economic growth of its member countries—Indonesia, Malaysia, the Philippines, Singapore, and Thailand—ASEAN markets have been recognized as among the brightest prospects in an otherwise stagnant world economy. Furthermore, ASEAN is regarded as the most important and promising effort at economic integration since the creation of the European Community. The political capacity of ASEAN has been demonstrated by its success in preventing the recognition of Kampuchea (formerly Cambodia) by the United Nations. Hence American policy toward the ASEAN countries is a proper focus of research attention.

Another reason for this study is that Japan is ASEAN's principal economic partner. Because the economies of Japan and the United States are becoming more directly competitive, the author's inquiry into how well American and Japanese firms perform in ASEAN will be useful in gauging the competitive position of the United States in the world economy and in judging the adequacy of U.S. policy in meeting the economic challenge of Japan.

This study is a natural extension of previous work by Lawrence B. Krause, a senior fellow in the Brookings Economic Studies program, that includes his contribution to *Asia's New Giant,* a book edited by Henry Rosovsky and Hugh Patrick that Brookings published in 1976, and his collaboration with Sueo Sekiguchi that led to the publication of *Economic Interaction in the Pacific Basin* by Brookings in 1980.

Among the many people who contributed advice in developing this study, the author particularly thanks Charles W. Robinson, chairman of the ASEAN-U.S. Business Council, and L. Oakley Johnson, its executive secretary. Through their efforts the author was able to gather much valuable information from the council. For helpful comments and suggestions, the author is grateful to Dwight D. Perkins, Hough T. Patrick, and Alfred Reifman.

Eric M. Leeper and Christine M. Ross provided research assistance and verified the factual content of the manuscript, which was edited by Caroline Lalire. The index was prepared by Florence Robinson.

This study was financed in part by the Ford Foundation, the Rockefeller Foundation, and the U.S. Department of State. The views expressed here are the author's alone and should not be ascribed to the organizations that supported the project financially, or to the trustees, officers, or other staff members of the Brookings Institution.

BRUCE K. MAC LAURY
President

June 1982
Washington, D.C.

Contents

Chapter One

Introduction

The United States has championed a global approach to international economic policy and has rarely evaluated the consequences of its policies for countries other than industrial ones. That approach was proper when the United States was the world's economic giant and when a few industrial countries dominated the world economy. But the United States is no longer in an economically preeminent position. Americans are no longer richer than many other peoples. Having a global economic policy based on the older industrial countries, when the developing countries are now the world's growth leaders, is no longer adequate for the United States. Such a policy engenders unnecessary costs and overlooks many opportunities. It also cannot meet the economic challenge of Japan.

The shortcomings of U.S. policy are greatest with respect to the advanced developing countries. Nowhere are these shortcomings more apparent than in the Pacific basin, particularly in dealing with the countries of the Association of Southeast Asian Nations (ASEAN)—the Republic of Indonesia, the Federation of Malaysia, the Republic of the Philippines, Singapore, and Thailand. Up till now, the United States has not taken the ASEAN countries properly into account in its policy, even though they are its fourth largest trading partner, after Canada, Japan, and the European Community.[1] We can and should remedy that deficiency. But we can do so only by becoming aware of specific country and regional issues and the impact of U.S. policy actions on them. This will also aid in meeting the Japanese challenge.

The Concept of the Japanese Challenge

It is widely recognized that the U.S. economy has performed badly in recent years. The growth in productivity has dwindled to almost nothing

1. U.S. Department of Commerce, International Trade Administration, *A Guide to Doing Business in the ASEAN Region* (Government Printing Office, 1981).

and both inflation and unemployment have increased substantially. Furthermore, in a fundamental sense the U.S. economy has not adapted to the reality of international interdependence—adjustments are not being made fast enough and opportunities are not being seized. In all these respects, Japan has had a much better performance. Thus half of the Japanese challenge to the United States is for us to reverse these trends and to become as economically successful as Japan. Why Japan? Because the Japanese have demonstrated how well an industrial country based on private enterprise can be managed. It is of little comfort to the United States that it has performed somewhat better than many European countries. Japan has shown that external shocks like the oil crises of the 1970s can be overcome without accommodating inflation or accepting high unemployment. Nothing inherent in the U.S. economy or society prevents similar successes.

The other half of the Japanese challenge is to make American business firms fully competitive with Japanese firms in world markets. As the Japanese economy has developed, it has become more competitive with and less complementary to the U.S. economy both in the goods and services it produces and sells to the world and in those it buys from others. Theory suggests that competition can be mutually beneficial if it spurs both parties to greater economic efficiency. When the process is working well, heightened competition leads to market-determined specialization along the lines of comparative advantage. However, theory does not suggest that a contestant that falters in the competitive race will benefit; indeed it might suffer in both a relative and an absolute sense.

If Japanese industry continues to develop its capacity, so that Japan becomes clearly superior to the United States in many advanced areas of manufacturing, it can by itself select those products in which it will expand. Industrial firms in the United States (and other countries) will then find that they are left to produce other goods, probably those for which demand is rising less rapidly, whose prospects for technical advance are less exciting, and which yield fewer profits and fewer high-paying jobs. Under this assumption, U.S. companies would find themselves below the technological frontier and in competition with producers from many countries. Hence U.S. export prices would be kept from rising through competition, its terms of trade would worsen, and its income growth would be reduced.

Contrast this situation with one in which U.S. industry is successful in meeting the Japanese challenge. American firms would be in the forefront of many (but not all) new technologies, which would result in new products and more efficient processes. American firms would earn high profits and be able to pay high wages. For them to do this, however, two conditions must be met. The firms must have the desire and the ability to devote large sums to research and development. And they must command a significant share of world markets. For many new technologies, a market larger than that provided from within the United States is necessary to achieve the economies of scale required to make research profitable. This need is already observed for such products as commercial airplanes and nuclear power plants and is likely to become more widespread with time. Furthermore, if American firms confine themselves to the domestic market, they will discover only too late that they have been overtaken by foreign competitors.

For most countries, to be economically second or third best is not a tragedy. Some societies may rationally choose leisure over work and present over future consumption. But such choices are not consistent with shouldering a heavy political and security burden. If world order and peace depend on the United States taking a superpower role, it must have a superpower economy to support that role.

The Scope of the Book

This study is about the economic interaction of the United States with the ASEAN countries. It is a subject worthy of attention for four reasons. First, the ASEAN countries are among the fastest growing countries in the world, and the lessons from their experience may provide a guide for other developing countries. Second, the institution of ASEAN is the most important economic and political effort at integration since the creation of the European Community and has the greatest chance of success of all such efforts among developing countries. Third, Japan is the dominant economic partner of the ASEAN countries, and the U.S. ability to compete there has implications for meeting the Japanese challenge throughout the world. Finally, the evaluation of U.S. economic policy in the ASEAN context provides insight into the usefulness and appropriateness of U.S. policy more generally.

The study begins with a brief history of ASEAN as an institution, a review of the economics of integration as it applies to ASEAN, and an examination of the economic policy initiatives of ASEAN. Chapter 3 provides a short description of the economies of the member countries, followed by a discussion of U.S. interest in those countries and of Japanese policies toward them. The economic involvement of ASEAN countries with the United States and Japan is analyzed in chapters 4 and 5. And in the last two chapters the policy issues and options of the United States are explored.

Chapter Two

The Institution of ASEAN

Just because of their rapid economic growth, Indonesia, Malaysia, the Philippines, Singapore, and Thailand would be worthy of special attention in evaluating the adequacy of U.S. international economic policy. That they have chosen to form ASEAN makes them doubly important.

Postwar history is strewn with failed efforts of developing countries to form institutions to promote economic integration. Some, like the East African Common Market, have disappeared without a trace. Others, like the Latin American Free Trade Association, have changed their names but are still empty shells. A high failure rate comes as no surprise, since economic integration is an intensely political act and few developing countries have sufficient domestic political strength to sustain the effort. Integration schemes are begun at the urging of certain political leaders or because of particular circumstances, but fade as those leaders are eclipsed or conditions change and the costs of integration become evident. The one real success at economic integration has been the European Community, and that occurred among advanced industrial countries (although the Community has been expanded to include some semi-industrial countries like Greece).

Why then should ASEAN be taken seriously? The answer is that in one crucial respect ASEAN is more like the European Community than any other integrative effort: it is held together by political fear. Walter Hallstein, the first president of the Community, frequently said that the common market was in politics, not in business. That is, the common market was primarily formed not to gain the considerable economic advantages envisioned, but to meet the political challenges of postwar Europe. A political solution to Franco-German animosity had to be found; a European effort to face up to the Soviet military-strategic challenge was a necessity; and a way to fend off American economic domination was considered essential. Although not the only factor, the European Community was important in achieving all these goals.

The ASEAN countries confront similar dangers. They all face threats to their internal order from insurgency movements supported from outside their countries; they all feel imperiled by the aggressive military thrust of Vietnam supported by the Soviet Union; some fear the latent power of Mainland China and the involvement of their ethnic Chinese minorities; and they all believe that Japan alone or in combination with the United States could dominate their economies. ASEAN can in part protect its members from these dangers.[1] And since these dangers are unlikely to subside, ASEAN will continue to be nurtured.

History

ASEAN was conceived in Bangkok, Thailand, in August 1967 to replace a rather ineffective institution, the Association of Southeast Asia, which had existed since 1961 for the limited purpose of promoting cordial relations among the newly independent countries of the region. The purpose of ASEAN, as specified in the Bangkok Declaration, is "to accelerate the economic growth, social progress and cultural development in the region through joint endeavour in the spirit of equality and partnership in order to strengthen the foundation for a prosperous and peaceful community of Southeast Asian nations; to promote regional peace and stability . . .; to promote active collaboration and mutual assistance on matters of common interest in the economic, social, cultural, technical, scientific and administrative fields; . . . to collaborate more effectively for the greater utilization of their agriculture and industries, the expansion of their trade including the study of problems of international commodity trade, the improvement of their transportation and communication facilities and the raising of the living standards of the peoples."[2] Thus ASEAN was to have a broader purpose than promoting economic well-being, although gaining prosperity was clearly a major goal.

Compared with other diplomatic efforts of this kind, ASEAN developed a low-keyed style. It avoided grand designs for fear of creating unrealistic expectations and of putting too much strain on the political structures of the member countries. Rather than provide for an impressive secretariat that would absorb scarce financial and human resources, the organization

1. Charles E. Morrison and Astri Suhrke, "ASEAN in Regional Defense and Development," in Sudershan Chawla and D. R. SarDesai, eds., *Changing Patterns of Security and Stability in Asia* (Praeger, 1980), pp. 192–214.

2. The Bangkok Declaration of ASEAN, as printed in *The ASEAN Report* (Hong Kong: Dow Jones, 1979), vol. 2, pp. 7–8.

assigned its duties to officials within national governments. While a number of ASEAN meetings were held and some other signs of life were evident, like joint conferences with other countries, it is neither unkind nor inaccurate to suggest that little was accomplished during ASEAN's first eight years of existence. What is remarkable is that it continued to exist at all given the continued political tensions among the member countries.

However, ASEAN did continue to exist and important personal contacts were established. Moreover, when the need arose, ASEAN was able to play a role in unifying the member countries. The need became evident after Saigon fell to the North Vietnamese in April 1975. Meeting in May, the ASEAN foreign ministers decided, at the urging of Indonesia, that the problems confronting the five countries were so vital that a conference of heads of state must be held. Preparations for the summit began as early as September 1975. They continued with a series of bilateral meetings among the member countries in January 1976, and relations intensified in February with meetings of economic ministers and with several bilateral summits. The first full ASEAN summit, held in Denpasar, Bali, February 23–25, 1976, was a tremendous success and, for many observers, marked the emergence of ASEAN as a functioning institution.

The Bali summit produced some formal documents, one of which, the Treaty of Amity and Cooperation in Southeast Asia (February 24, 1976), had been under discussion for some time but needed to be completed by the heads of state. The treaty, which implicitly replaced the Bangkok Declaration, established the general principles for relations among ASEAN countries, including a procedure for settlement of disputes. It pointedly stated that the purpose of ASEAN included the strengthening of the national security and resiliency of the member countries to preserve their respective national identities.

Another summit document, the Declaration of ASEAN Concord (February 24, 1976), attempted to increase the economic role of ASEAN. It called for the elevation of economic matters to the same status as political and social ones. Regular meetings of economic ministers were initiated to parallel those of the foreign ministers. Furthermore, it adopted in general terms an action program in economics that included cooperation on basic commodities such as food and energy, support for industrial projects in each of the ASEAN countries, and promotion of intra-ASEAN trade, in part through preferential trading arrangements. These plans were given more substance in a meeting of economic ministers the following month. Also as part of the Bali summit, provision was made for a modest but permanent secretariat of the institution to be located in Jakarta, the capital of Indonesia.

While the pace of ASEAN activity picked up after the Bali summit, actual accomplishments of ASEAN as an institution are still hard to document. Working by the principle of consensus, it progresses at the pace of its most reluctant member. Often Indonesia has been the least willing to take significant economic measures within ASEAN, although none of the countries has questioned the value of the institution itself. When interest in ASEAN began to wane, new external threats brought it back into focus. These threats have included the arrival of refugees from Vietnam, the invasion of Kampuchea (formerly Cambodia) by Vietnam, the attack on Vietnam by China, the flow of refugees from Kampuchea to Thailand, and disturbances along the Thai-Kampuchean border. Thus the glue holding ASEAN together has been constantly reapplied.

Economic Benefits

While politics makes ASEAN possible, economic benefits will be necessary if the institution is to mature and grow. Theory suggests that economic gains can be achieved through economic integration among independent countries. The gains are of two kinds, static and dynamic. The static gains arise from redirecting markets and reorganizing production from existing productive facilities and other factors of production; the dynamic gains come from expanding facilities, improving efficiency, and increasing economic growth. In developing countries, the prospects for dynamic gains are significantly greater than for static ones. Countries are good candidates for integration if their economies are actually competitive but potentially complementary. The particular measures adopted as part of ASEAN and the circumstances of the member countries will determine the magnitude of the gains and their distribution among the individual members. These factors will also determine how nonmember countries will be affected by ASEAN integration. In general, the more that dynamic gains dominate static gains, the more likely that nonmembers will benefit from ASEAN.

Dynamic gains stem from a number of economic forces. The growth of international trade among member countries results in larger markets for business firms, which can then capture economies of scale when investing in new productive capacity. Increased trade also leads to greater specialization among enterprises and thus to greater division of labor. It generates a spirit of enterprise and improves the quality of competition, which in turn improves efficiency and growth. Finally, an integrative effort can improve the terms of trade of member countries in its trade with nonmembers, thereby increasing the real incomes of members. Securing these dynamic gains will require a rise in business investment as a share of gross national product, or an increase in output per unit of input, or, preferably, a combination of both.

The amount of gain and its distribution among member countries depend on six variables.[3]

The size of the market. The larger the potential market created through integration, the larger the gain. The total population of ASEAN countries is 250.6 million (mid-1979), which implies considerable potential market size. Enlarging the market will not bring as much gain to Indonesia, which alone has 57 percent of the ASEAN population, as it will to the other four, especially Singapore. Therefore Singapore could improve its terms of trade through higher export prices if it had better access to a much larger market.

Preintegration degree of inefficiency. The more trade barriers and other distortions that existed in member countries before integration, the more scope there is for improvement and the greater the possible efficiency gain. While quantitative comparisons are difficult to make, ASEAN countries did not have particularly distorting policies by the standards of other developing countries, even though in reality much distortion exists. Indonesia probably has the most to gain from reducing distortions, followed by the Philippines, Thailand, and Malaysia. Few benefits from this source are open to Singapore, which already has achieved relatively free trade.

Preintegration barriers of trading partners. Because of economic structure and location, countries have natural trading partners. The degree to which the natural markets of a country are closed to it by trade barriers that are subsequently removed by economic integration is a variable similar to, but distinct from, the inefficiency variable noted above. It is important in determining the distribution of gains among members rather than in calculating the size of the total gain. The countries with the most distorting policies were Indonesia, the Philippines, and Thailand.

Geographical position. Countries that are physically close to one another gain more from integration than those that are not. And when nations

3. For a more detailed description and measurement of variables as they applied to Europe, see Lawrence B. Krause, *European Economic Integration and the United States* (Brookings Institution, 1968), chap. 2.

share a landmass, they gain more if they have a common border than if they do not. Although this variable relates primarily to efficiency of transportation of goods and people, it also involves the ease of information flow that comes from being located in the same time zone, within reach of the same radio transmitter, and so forth. The ASEAN countries are close to one another and should benefit from their propinquity.

Preintegration economic conditions and policies. The gains accruing to countries from integration in part reflect the preexisting state of their economies. The worse the preexisting mismanagement that is corrected by integration, the greater the potential gains. If, for instance, a country that has discouraged saving and investment by domestic or foreign enterprises changes this policy because it is inconsistent with obligations or expectations under ASEAN, the gains could be substantial. But since measuring this variable involves examining tax structures, government expenditure patterns, monetary policies, regulation, and administrative skills, among other things, it is almost impossible to do with any precision.

Integrative policies and firmness of commitment. The gains from integration also depend on the degree to which laws and practices that differentiate among member countries are removed. In the ideal situation, goods, services, and factors of production would move between member countries as if they were one country. The closer the actual situation is to the ideal, the more the gain. Equally important, however, is the firmness of the commitment to change. It is better for ASEAN to recommend modest policies that are actually adopted and fully accepted by member countries than a far-reaching and demanding program that will not be accepted or will not survive under stress. ASEAN's success has come from slow, incremental developments, and ASEAN may be not only the best plan but the only feasible one for the future.

The variables important in determining the gains from economic integration are the same ones that help explain why a strategy of export promotion encourages growth much more than a strategy of import substitution.[4] Thus the essence of economic integration may be its ability to push member countries into export promotion and away from import substitution. If so, regional economic integration appears to be a second-best alternative to global free trade, and possibly a more achievable one.

4. Anne O. Krueger, "Export-Led Industrial Growth Reconsidered," in Wontack Hong and Lawrence B. Krause, eds., *Trade and Growth of the Advanced Developing Countries in the Pacific Basin* (Seoul: Korea Development Institute, 1981), pp. 3–34.

Policies

Two kinds of policies have been adopted by ASEAN to promote economic integration: highly visible or showcase policies and unheralded or invisible ones. The natural tendency is to judge the success of ASEAN efforts only by the showcase policies. But it would be misleading to do so.

The three ASEAN policies that have attracted most attention in member countries and abroad are ASEAN industrial projects, preferential trading arrangements, and industrial complementation agreements. Such showcase policies are necessary, many believe, because continued political support for ASEAN depends on having tangible evidence that the organization is bringing about economic progress. This view is of doubtful validity. Public support for ASEAN depends on the continuation of external threats, not on the capturing of economic gains. Nevertheless, if ASEAN policies are undertaken that force member countries to incur costs, commensurate benefits must be forthcoming to prevent disenchantment with the effort at integration.

Industrial Projects

The policy of promoting ASEAN industrial projects, the epitome of a showcase policy, was taken up at the Bali summit and was specified in detail at a meeting of economic ministers in March 1976. It was thought that an industrial project could be designed large enough to capture economies of scale if the entire ASEAN market, rather than just a national one, were served. The idea is similar to one adopted earlier by the Central American Common Market, in which each country was guaranteed one integration industry. In practice that scheme did not work because of the reluctance of investors to commit themselves to certain very undeveloped countries. The ASEAN idea is conceptually better, since monopoly status is not being offered to the selected projects. However, by the same token, there is little advantage accruing to the project by being designated. ASEAN did make an interesting innovation by offering 10 percent equity participation to the ASEAN countries other than the host country. Thus, if fully implemented, the host country would own only 60 percent of the project, with the remaining equity being shared equally by the others. Five projects—one for each country—were tentatively selected, pending the outcome of feasibility studies.[5] The idea was given encouragement by the

5. The five projects were urea fertilizer in Indonesia and Malaysia, superphosphates in the

Japanese in August 1977, when Prime Minister Takeo Fukuda promised financial support of $1 billion if the studies established the economic viability of the projects.

The effort has not been completely successful. Some progress has been made in the projects for Indonesia and Malaysia. Detailed plans for the Thai rock-salt and soda-ash project were approved by the economic ministers of the ASEAN countries at their meeting in January 1982.[6] However, the original projects for the Philippines and Singapore have been abandoned. The problem with the Philippine project is presumably related to the cost-effectiveness of the investment and thus to its economic feasibility. A subsequent proposal for a pulp and paper plant for the Philippines was also set aside. But at the January 1982 meeting, plans for a copper fabrication project in the Philippines were tentatively approved, pending the working out of detailed plans. The Singapore case is more complex, since it involved a manufactured product (diesel engines). The project was dropped because Indonesia was also encouraging investment in the same product. Singapore has proposed no alternative. Furthermore, Singapore has chosen to minimize its equity participation in other countries (1 percent rather than 10 percent) because of its general disillusionment with the policy. Thus the projects are now 60 percent owned by the host country, 13 percent each by the other three, and only 1 percent by Singapore.

Any industrial investment that was already set to be undertaken could of course be designated as the ASEAN industrial project, as was the urea fertilizer project in Indonesia, but this circumvents the intention of the program, which is to increase total investment, not just to rename it. But how can a project that would not otherwise be undertaken be made feasible by being made an ASEAN industrial project? The output from designated projects is automatically granted trade preferences within ASEAN, but, as discussed below, the preference margin is not that large and many other products are also granted trade preferences; thus the preference could not be a determining factor. Furthermore, exporting to world markets is usually a better alternative than relying on even a protected ASEAN market. Financing is assured for ASEAN industrial projects, but if all other factors

---

Philippines, diesel engines in Singapore, and soda ash in Thailand. These suggested projects grew out of a study conducted by the Department of Economic and Social Affairs of the UN Secretariat, "Economic Co-operation among Member Countries of the Association of Southeast Asian Nations" (the Robinson Report), published in the *Journal of Development Planning*, no. 7 (New York: United Nations, 1974).

6. *Asian Wall Street Journal Weekly*, January 25, 1982, p. 16.

are positive, a shortage of finance seldom stops an industrial project, given the development of capital markets in the region.[7]

The impression is unavoidable that those ASEAN projects that have gone forward would have been undertaken anyway; the ASEAN symbolism was merely attached to a national development effort. Making use of such symbols is not unusual or reprehensible; however, it may be counterproductive if it politicizes an investment decision that would otherwise be made on economic grounds, by satisfying market tests of efficiency. And if an ASEAN project should ultimately fail, the failure will have political implications that will hurt the institution itself.

Trade Preferences

The second showcase policy provides for the creation of trade preferences for member countries as established by the Agreement on ASEAN Preferential Trading Arrangements (February 24, 1977). Although many specific inducements are provided—including promotion of long-term contracts for commodities among member countries, trade credits at preferential interest rates, preferences for supplying government contracts, and liberalization of nontariff barriers on a preferential basis—the principal measure is preferential reductions in tariffs. Each member country selects its own products for which preferential reductions of tariffs are intended, and the members jointly decide on how many such items there will be.

The first batch of tariff preferences became effective in January 1978 and comprised 71 products—approximately 14 for each country—for which a preferential margin equal to 10 percent of the existing tariff was given to other member countries. A country could count as one of its 14 products a five-year guaranteed binding of a zero tariff rate on a product, a concession of particular importance to Singapore given its free trade status. Another 755 items were included in September 1978 and another 500 in March 1979. Further negotiations have added many new products, so that by the end of 1981, 7,000 items were receiving preferred tariff reductions of between 10 and 35 percent.[8] Still another 1,948 products were added in January 1982. Duties on items with less than $1 million of trade are to be 20 to 25 percent less than the duties on similar non-ASEAN products.[9]

7. The same may not apply to large-scale natural resource projects.
8. U.S. Department of Commerce, International Trade Administration, *A Guide to Doing Business in the ASEAN Region* (Government Printing Office, 1981), p. 8.
9. *Asian Wall Street Journal Weekly*, January 25, 1982, p. 16.

Although some of these tariff reductions may become meaningful, they have not yet done so.[10]

A basic difficulty arises from the product-by-product approach to tariff reductions, the approach used unsuccessfully by the Latin American Free Trade Association. At a minimum it is cumbersome and laborious, requiring lengthy negotiations in order to evaluate offers. It also imposes a significant administrative burden on governments. Furthermore, the political costs of trade liberalization for governments are maximized, since they must choose the industries to be "sacrificed." Domestic pressures will build up by the firms adversely affected. If the pressures become strong enough, the whole process can be stalled, as happened in the Latin America association. Even if many items are selected, the most sensitive ones will be withheld. But some countries, especially Indonesia, are reluctant to adopt an alternative, the so-called across-the-board approach used successfully by the European Community. They are unwilling to open their markets to external competition because they are at an early stage of industrialization, particularly compared with Singapore, and fear that their manufactures cannot compete with those of the more advanced members. Nevertheless, the across-the-board approach is much better because it covers all products; and it is preferable to accept a slow pace of trade liberalization by having just small margins of preference than the political costs and economic distortions that come from an item-by-item approach.

Complementation Schemes

The third showcase policy is the establishment of complementation schemes among private firms in the same industry in all member countries. These schemes might become important because they are linked to the more mundane developments described below. The purpose of complementation agreements is to enable already existing enterprises in an industry to become more efficient by specializing in certain particular product lines while giving up others and thereby to gain economies of scale.[11] To

10. Seiji Naya estimated that the early rounds of ASEAN tariff preferences could in time stimulate between $30 million and $50 million of trade. Seiji Naya, *ASEAN Trade Development and Cooperation: Preferential Trading Arrangements and Trade Liberalization*, Report to the UNCTAD, UNDP, and UNESCAP, Project RAS/77/015/A/40 (New York: United Nations, 1980), p. 50.

11. H. Edward English, "ASEAN's Quest for Allocative Efficiency in Manufacturing: Perspectives on the Role of Complementation and Trade Policies," in Ross Garnaut, ed., *ASEAN in a Changing Pacific and World Economy* (Miami: Australian National University Press, 1980), pp. 101–37.

qualify, production facilities must exist in at least four of the five member countries. Tariff preferences would automatically be granted to products from such facilities. As of 1982, only one agreement has been signed, for automobile components, but it appears significant enough to be attracting the attention of foreign firms, including American ones. It actually began operations on January 1, 1982. Under this pact, the ASEAN countries will cut tariffs in half and provide other concessional terms to a package of auto parts produced in the region.[12] The success of this ASEAN innovation is hard to forecast; it does run some risk of reducing needed competition among different business firms.

Unheralded Policies

By way of contrast, the invisible and unannounced policies of ASEAN may well be more significant in promoting trade. These policies include the formation of ASEAN associations of businessmen, bankers, professionals, and others. The governments encouraged the formation of the ASEAN Chambers of Commerce and Industry in 1972 to promote closer cooperation among the private sectors of the member countries. By 1981 this organization had established nineteen regional industry and commodity clubs.[13] Such clubs could lead to complementation agreements, but are important in promoting trade and investment even in their absence.

In addition, the ASEAN Banking Council established the ASEAN Finance Corporation in June 1981. This institution, created with $50 million of capital from bankers from all five ASEAN countries, intends to act like a regional merchant bank. It plans to underwrite debt and equity issues for ASEAN-based industries, serve as a conduit of capital to the ASEAN countries from other countries and international financial institutions, help promote partnerships between ASEAN and foreign industrial firms, and even assist in the creation of management for ASEAN-based companies.[14]

12. The original list of parts under the pact are diesel engines of 85 to 135 horsepower made in Indonesia; spokes, nipples, and drive chains for motorcycles and timing chains for cars from Malaysia; body panels for cars from the Philippines; body panels for light trucks from Thailand; and universal joints from Singapore. *Asian Wall Street Journal Weekly*, January 25, 1982, p. 16.

13. The fourteen industrial product clubs are automobiles, chemicals, cement, electrical and electronic products, rubber-based goods, agricultural machinery, food processing, furniture, iron and steel, pulp and paper, glass, ceramics, plywood, and textiles. Additional clubs are planned for leather, shipbuilding, cordage rope, twine and net, nonelectrical machinery, and nonferrous metal industries.

14. Presentation of H. Omar Abdalla, chairman of the ASEAN Finance Corporation, on

It has already formed a cooperative body with Japanese bankers called the ASEAN Development Corporation, which no doubt will help create new industrial investments in ASEAN countries.

Furthermore, the governments of the ASEAN countries have made efforts to reduce transportation and communication costs and to unify and simplify government forms, regulations and procedures, and the like. Such policies, which reduce the cost of information concerning markets and business opportunities in member countries, were notably successful in Latin America and are likely to be so in ASEAN. Thus intra-ASEAN trade promotion is not dependent on the explicit showcase policies, which may not be well-designed, but can develop in time through the evolution of better-working markets in the area as well as through generalized trade liberalization.

November 18, 1981, at the First ASEAN-U.S. Finance Conference in Kuala Lumpur, Malaysia.

Chapter Three

The ASEAN Countries
and the Outside World

The ASEAN countries are dynamic, rapidly changing countries. Gains in economic well-being have been substantial during the last fifteen years, and while income distribution is a serious problem in three of the member countries, at least some of the benefits of growth have reached the poorest members of society. The ASEAN countries have been experiencing what can be described as a peaceful and orderly revolution. Dramatic changes have occurred in their political, social, and cultural life. In addition, their governments have embarked on a course aimed at economic integration among the five countries—a complicated and demanding political activity.

This combination of internal and external change presents a challenge to all countries that desire to have peaceful relations with ASEAN countries. The challenge to others is to understand, to encourage, and indeed to benefit themselves from what is happening. The challenge may be greater for the United States than for Japan. The United States knows less about the ASEAN countries than Japan does and has had less experience in dealing with them. Indeed, for many years ASEAN and the ASEAN countries have received particular attention both from the Japanese government and from Japanese business.[1] Yet the United States may have more to gain from these countries and more to offer them.

The ASEAN Economies

In 1979 the sum of the gross domestic products of the five ASEAN countries was about $135 billion, only 6 percent of U.S. income in that year (table 3-1). However, the region's population of 251 million in 1979 is larger than that of the United States. The resulting per capita income of

---

1. Bernard K. Gordon, "Japan, the United States, and Southeast Asia," *Foreign Affairs*, vol. 56 (April 1978), pp. 579–600.

Table 3-1. *Salient Features of the Economies of ASEAN Countries*

Country	Popula-tion, mid-1979 (millions)	Total GDP, 1979 (millions of U.S. dollars)	GNP per capita, 1979 (U.S. dollars)	Average annual growth of GDP, 1970-79 (percent)	Adult literacy rate, 1976 (percent)	Life expectancy at birth (years)
Indonesia	142.9	49,210	370	7.6	62	53
Malaysia	13.1	20,340	1,370	7.9	60[a]	68
Philippines	46.7	29,380	600	6.2	88[a]	62
Singapore	2.4	9,010	3,830	8.4	75[b]	71
Thailand	45.5	27,640	590	7.7	84	62
ASEAN	250.6	135,580	538	. . .	. . .	. . .

Source: World Bank, *World Development Report, 1981* (Oxford University Press, 1981), pp. 134–35, 136–37, 138–39.
a. For years before 1976.
b. For years before 1975.

ASEAN was rather low by advanced developing country standards, only about $540 (1979 dollars). This economic snapshot as of 1979, though, is deceptive. It fails to reflect the rapid progress made in recent years, as seen in the nearly 8 percent annual growth rate during the 1970s, and the prospect for future gains.[2]

Two notable characteristics of ASEAN countries are their diverse income levels and the negative relationship that exists between size of population and per capita income. Indonesia is by far the largest country in aggregate GDP and population, but its per capita income is the lowest, $370 a year; in contrast, Singapore is the smallest country, with the highest per capita income, $3,830. Malaysia, the second smallest, has the second highest per capita income, $1,370. The Philippines and Thailand, which are about equal in population, both have incomes per capita of approximately $600.

Singapore

For the ASEAN countries, income per capita indicates quite well their degree of industrialization or modernization. Singapore is an advanced

2. The need to use market exchange rates to compare incomes of different countries also adds to the deceptiveness of the measure. In general, the income level of developing countries is higher in real purchasing power than market valuations suggest. See Irving B. Kravis, Alan Heston, and Robert Summers, *International Comparisons of Real Product and Purchasing Power*, UN International Comparison Project: Phase II (Johns Hopkins University Press, 1978).

Table 3-2. *Structure of the Production of ASEAN Countries, 1979*
Percent

	Agriculture		Industry				Services	
			Total		Manufacturing			
Country	Share of GDP	Average annual growth, 1970–79	Share of GDP	Average annual growth, 1970–79	Share of GDP	Average annual growth, 1970–79	Share of GDP	Average annual growth, 1970–79
Indonesia	30	3.6	33	11.3	9	12.5	37	9.2
Malaysia	24	5.0	33	9.9	16	12.4	43	8.4
Philippines	24	4.9	35	8.4	24	6.7	41	5.4
Singapore	2	1.7	36	8.6	28	9.3	62	8.5
Thailand	26	5.4	28	10.4	19	11.4	46	7.7

Source: Same as table 3-1.

country by almost any criterion. Since achieving independence in 1965, it has grown from an entrepôt and a service center into an industrial country as well. As seen in table 3-2, the largest source of Singapore's income is services, reflecting the nature of the city-state and the development of its economy. Within services, those yielding low income, like retail and wholesale trade, have been declining, while those yielding high income, like finance, insurance, and real estate, have been rising.[3] In addition, manufacturing has grown particularly fast and now provides about one-quarter of the GDP. In manufacturing there has been a movement, encouraged by the government, from labor-intensive to more skill-intensive industry.

Singapore has always strongly supported ASEAN in the belief that the institution could help solve the economic and social problems of the region, that Singapore's own manufacturers would be major beneficiaries of trade liberalization, and that the country itself would prosper from being a regional service center.[4] It also recognized that ASEAN membership would tend to moderate the deep-seated political and social antagonisms between Singapore and its ASEAN neighbors. As an ethnic Chinese city among countries in which Chinese minorities are resented, feared, sometimes discriminated against, and sometimes subjected to violence, Singapore wants

3. Chia Siow Yue, "Singapore's Trade and Development Strategy, and ASEAN Economic Co-operation, with Special Reference to the ASEAN Common Approach to Foreign Economic Relations," in Ross Garnaut, ed., *ASEAN in a Changing Pacific and World Economy* (Miami: Australian National University Press, 1980), pp. 241–79.

4. Robert L. Rau, "The Role of Singapore in ASEAN," *Contemporary Southeast Asia*, vol. 3 (September 1981), pp. 99–112.

to establish good and cooperative working relations with its neighbors. But it recognizes that its support for ASEAN must be low-keyed lest it be accused of trying to exercise too much influence on events and policies. This fear, however, has not inhibited it from being an internal critic of the ASEAN policies with which it disagrees.

Republic of the Philippines

The country with the second highest share of industry in domestic output is the Philippines, which also obtains about one-quarter of its GDP from manufacturing. Agriculture, however, is still somewhat larger than manufacturing and has been inching up in recent years as more resources have been directed to rural development. Indeed, growth of agricultural output has been very high in all ASEAN countries except Singapore. Since 1973, construction has been the fastest growing sector in the Philippine economy, because both mining and manufacturing were hindered by the rise of oil prices.[5]

Although individual Filipino statesmen like Carlos Romulo played an important role in ASEAN's creation and development, the Philippines remains somewhat indifferent to ASEAN. Its geographical separation from the other countries seems to limit its attachment to them. And there is little evidence that ASEAN membership has influenced Philippine industrial policy or development in any significant way. While there is no active opposition in the Philippines to ASEAN membership, neither is there evidence of strong commitment to it.

Federation of Malaysia

Industrialization has also reached a fairly high level in Malaysia as a result of growth in recent years. Manufacturing in particular has expanded rapidly, although it is still only 16 percent of gross domestic product. The share of Malaysia's income coming from agriculture is about 25 percent of GDP and is thought to have great potential for expansion. Malaysia remains the world's largest producer of natural rubber and palm oil. Meanwhile, energy production is becoming more important, having expanded at

5. Romeo M. Bautista, "Trade Strategies and Industrial Development in the Philippines: With Special Reference to Region Trade Preferences," in Garnaut, ed., *ASEAN in a Changing Pacific and World Economy*, pp. 175–201.

a 27.1 percent annual rate between 1974 and 1978. Malaysia is a net exporter of energy and has substantial potential for further development.

Malyasia has had strained relations with three of its ASEAN neighbors: with Indonesia after Malaysia gained its independence in 1963; with the Philippines, which tried to reestablish a long-standing claim to Sabah; and with Singapore because of the two countries' political separation in 1965. As a result, Malaysia played a limited role in the early years of ASEAN. But with the passage of time and the strengthening of its sovereignty, Malaysia has become more actively involved. Nevertheless, it is likely to defer to Indonesia on most policies related to ASEAN and is not likely to suggest initiatives of its own.

Thailand

The Thai economy has undergone significant changes in recent years. The country has had more than its share of external disturbances, the result of its proximity to Indochina. Also, the domestic political scene has been unstable, with frequent changes of leadership. Yet the economy has performed quite well. There has been a sharp decline in the share of GDP coming from agriculture, despite very satisfactory growth of agriculture and significant diversification of crops responding to market signals. Industry has expanded and manufacturing now accounts for close to 20 percent of GDP. Energy is a major concern for the economy. The country until recently has been dependent on imported petroleum for 80 percent of its energy needs and has therefore been seriously affected by increases in petroleum prices. But natural gas has been discovered and promises to become the main source of energy for the country fairly soon. Furthermore, some evidence of petroleum reserves has been found that could prove to be of commercial size.

Thailand has been one of the most enthusiastic supporters of ASEAN and was instrumental in its creation. Much of the original administrative work for the organization was done in Bangkok. Given Thailand's exposed position next to Indochina, its search for institutionalized friendship is easily understood.

Republic of Indonesia

Indonesia is the ASEAN country that has the furthest to go to complete its modernization. Industry has grown rapidly as a share of GDP, but mainly because of the mining of petroleum, whose benefits have not effectively spread to the rest of the economy. Manufacturing constitutes less that 10 percent of the economy, but is growing rapidly. As an indication of Indonesia's lack of development, it has been estimated that electricity consumption per capita is less in Indonesia than even in Mainland China, though used more efficiently than in China.[6] Overall, however, economic growth has been rapid and the prospects for the future are also promising. Indonesia will remain a petroleum exporter for some time. Other natural resources are also available for development. And although the timing is uncertain, eventually the manufacturing sector of Indonesia will evolve.

Indonesia took much of the initiative in forming ASEAN and views itself as the natural leader of the organization. However, Indonesia considers itself not just an ASEAN country. With the fifth largest population in the world, it sees itself as having a world role. Thus Indonesia is of critical importance to ASEAN, but possibly ASEAN is not to Indonesia.

International Involvement

Compared with either developed or developing countries elsewhere, all the ASEAN countries have a high level of international involvement. Among the ASEAN countries themselves, however, international involvement ranges from moderate to remarkably high. The ranking of the countries differs according to which elements are considered, but in general one can say that the Philippines has the least, and Singapore the most, international involvement.

Merchandise Trade

International trade of merchandise is of great significance to all the ASEAN countries. As seen in table 3-3, exports of goods and nonfactor services (other than interest and dividends) constitute 19 percent of the GDP of the Philippines in 1979, 58 percent of Malaysia's, and an astounding 187 percent of Singapore's. Exports can have greater value than the total GDP if the import content of exports is very large, as is the case in Singapore. No other country in the world can compare with Singapore in this respect; even Hong Kong's exports are less than 100 percent of GDP. Indeed, there are only a few countries where percentages of exports are as

6. Peter McCawley, "Comment," in ibid., pp. 233–38.

Table 3-3. *International Trade of ASEAN Countries, 1979*

Country	Merchandise trade (millions of U.S. dollars)		Average annual growth of real exports, 1970–79 (percent)	Exports of goods and nonfactor services as percent of GDP
	Exports	Imports		
Indonesia	15,590	7,225	6.5	30
Malaysia	11,077	7,849	6.5	58
Philippines	4,601	6,613	6.2	19
Singapore	14,233	17,635	11.0	187
Thailand	5,288	7,190	12.0	23
ASEAN	50,789	46,512	...	...

Source: World Bank, *World Development Report, 1981*, pp. 142–43, 148–49.

high as Malaysia's. The comparable figure for the United States is 9 percent and for Japan 12 percent. Since the ASEAN countries have such an important external orientation, their economies are particularly sensitive to external factors.

Manufactured products (excluding refined petroleum) constitute about 60 percent of ASEAN imports and are the major component of imports of all five countries. However, ASEAN exports contain only 22 percent manufactured goods; and Singapore alone is primarily a manufactured goods exporter (particularly if refined petroleum products are included). At 1977 prices, fuels constituted 20 percent of ASEAN imports and 34 percent of exports; these percentages will be higher following the price increases of 1979–80. The fact that ASEAN countries are a net exporter of energy is of great advantage, since energy supplies can be guaranteed among the member countries. Indonesia is the principal producer and exporter, although Malaysia is also a net exporter. Singapore, a large exporter of refined petroleum products, is an even larger importer of crude petroleum. The Philippines and Thailand have been large net importers of fuels; but because Thailand has discovered large domestic sources of energy, its situation will change. ASEAN is also a net supplier of food, primarily because of production in Thailand and, to a lesser extent, in the Philippines. Indonesia, Malaysia, and Singapore are all net importers of food, with Indonesia being the world's largest rice importer. ASEAN is a large provider of other raw materials to the world. Indeed, it provides the world with 91 percent of its natural rubber, 87 percent of its tin, 88 percent of its palm oil, 73 percent

Table 3-4. *Geographic Distribution of the Merchandise Trade of ASEAN Countries, 1979*

Percent

	Exports			Imports		
Originating country	ASEAN	United States	Japan	ASEAN	United States	Japan
Indonesia	14.2	20.4	46.1	11.6	14.6	29.2
Malaysia	20.1	17.3	23.4	14.5	15.0	22.4
Philippines	4.1	30.2	26.4	5.8	23.0	22.6
Singapore	24.0	13.8	9.6	28.4	14.3	17.0
Thailand	16.7	11.2	21.2	7.5	15.7	25.7

Source: International Monetary Fund, *Direction of Trade Statistics Yearbook, 1981.*

of its copra, 62 percent of its tropical hardwood, and most of its spices, plus some copper, abaca, and cocoa.[7]

The analysis of ASEAN's trade pattern (table 3-4) is difficult because trade statistics by destination are not accurately reported by the member countries.[8] A great deal of smuggling exists, especially into Indonesia and the Philippines—countries with relatively high trade barriers and thousands of miles of coastline that are difficult to patrol. The recorded data indicate that in absolute amounts intra-ASEAN exports increased from less than $1 billion in 1967 to $8.9 billion in 1979. Nevertheless, it appears as if intra-ASEAN trade has been declining as a share of total ASEAN trade. In the 1966–68 period exports to other members constituted 19.1 percent of ASEAN exports, but the share fell to 16.8 percent after a decade of ASEAN existence (1976–79). Of course ASEAN efforts to promote intra-ASEAN trade were introduced only at the end of the period and thus could not possibly show any results. Even so, the relative decline in that trade is disturbing for the future of ASEAN, since many observers will judge ASEAN's success by this measure.

Several factors may account for the decline. It may simply reflect the

7. Keynote address by the Honorable 'Ele Dato' Seri Dr. Mahathir Bin Mohamad, prime minister of Malaysia, at the ASEAN-U.S. Economic Conference in the Kuala Lumpur Hilton, November 18, 1981.

8. Large errors are known to exist. Singapore's exports to Indonesia have not been reported by Singapore since the mid-1960s. Entrepôt trade may have been reported asymmetrically. In general, large discrepancies appear in the bilateral reporting of the trade flows by the member countries. Seiji Naya, *ASEAN Trade Development and Cooperation: Preferential Trading Arrangements and Trade Liberalization*, Report of the UNCTAD, UNDP, and UNESCAP, Project RAS/77/015/A/40 (New York: United Nations, 1980).

decreasing importance of Singapore's entrepôt trade. Or perhaps the primary product specialization of the members lacks complementarity in structure, even though food and energy is traded intensively among them. Alternatively, the explanation could be the pull of large markets in the developed countries, reinforced by aid and loan-tying by them. Also possibly the import-substitution policies of the member countries were biased against regional trade.[9] Whatever the causes, they must be overcome to help sustain ASEAN as an institution. And in fact the intra-ASEAN share of trade has risen for most member countries in more recent years.

Service Trade

The international trade of services is also important to ASEAN countries, particularly Singapore. In Singapore two-thirds of all employment is in services, which are largely export-oriented.[10] Singapore continues to provide foreigners with a wide range of services, including those of wholesale and retail trade, restaurants and hotels, and transportation and communication, as well as financial, insurance, and other business services. In recent years Singapore has earned a service surplus in its balance of payments of over $3 billion. The Philippines has also been a supplier of financial and construction services to foreigners, and all the ASEAN countries have been important tourist centers.

Foreign Investment

The ASEAN countries are also major recipients of international capital resources and view themselves as having access to world capital markets. As seen in table 3-5, during recent years net capital inflows have amounted to about $5 billion a year (4 billion special drawing rights). Approximately one-third of this amount came from direct foreign investment, one-third from official sources, and the remaining third from portfolio and short-term capital. The total value of direct foreign investment in ASEAN countries amounted to over $16 billion at the end of 1979, which is a modest proportion of total world foreign investment, but not an insignificant one. Almost half of this amount is invested in Indonesia, principally in petroleum production and other mining ventures. One-quarter is invested in Singapore in

9. Ibid., pp. 15–26.
10. Greg F. H. Seow, "The Service Sector in Singapore's Economy: Performance and Structure," *Malayan Economic Review*, vol. 24 (October 1979), pp. 46–73.

Table 3-5. *Current Account Balance and International Capital Flows of ASEAN Countries, 1977–80*

Billions of U.S. dollars

Year	Current account balance	Direct investment in ASEAN	Portfolio and other private investment	Official loans and transfers[a]
1977	-1.9	1.3	2.7	1.7
1978	-4.2	1.7	2.9	1.9
1979	-2.5	2.0	4.2	2.2
1980	-3.3	2.8	4.9	2.5

Sources: *International Financial Statistics*, vol. 25 (April 1982); and World Bank, *World Debt Tables, 1981* (Washington, D.C.: World Bank, 1981).
a. Includes both bilateral and multilateral sources.

manufacturing and petroleum refining, and the other 26 percent is spread among Malaysia (14 percent), the Philippines (8 percent), and Thailand (4 percent). All the countries welcome foreign investment, subject to various restraints as well as incentives. For Singapore direct investment has been the critical element in the industrialization process and figures prominently in future plans. Access to international credit has also been essential to the Philippines, which has had to borrow large amounts to cover its balance-of-payments deficit, caused by the rise in oil prices. To a lesser extent, this is also true of Thailand.

Summary

Like most developing countries in the 1960s, ASEAN countries tried to stimulate industrialization through the strategy of import substitution. Protection for domestic manufacturing varied in the member countries from quite moderate in Singapore to quite severe in Indonesia. But unlike many other developing countries, the ASEAN countries have recognized the limitations of the strategy. Toward the end of the 1960s, Singapore was already moving toward export promotion and import liberalization. Malaysia followed a similar though more restrained path. Indonesia, the Philippines, and Thailand recognize the value of export promotion but have been less vigorous in liberalizing import protections of various sorts; on balance, they may still be penalizing exports. For Indonesia import liberalization is at an early stage. On the whole, the experience with export promotion has been encouraging, and the commitment of ASEAN countries to further integration with the world economy seems likely.

U.S. Interests

Although the rest of this study is chiefly devoted to the many facets of the large and growing economic interest of the United States in ASEAN countries, more is involved. The United States has strategic, political, and even ideologic interests in ASEAN countries and in ASEAN as an institution. The United States has every reason to pursue those interests with vigor and understanding. The ASEAN countries expect it to do so, and they certainly interpret U.S. actions as efforts to promote U.S. interests. Success for the United States, however, need not be at the expense of the ASEAN countries, since the basic U.S. desire for peace and prosperity in the region is not in conflict with the interests of the countries themselves.

In strategic and political terms, it is important to recognize that four great powers—the United States, the Soviet Union, China, and Japan—meet and contend in ASEAN territory. The global confrontation between the United States and the Soviet Union is not played out directly in the area, but elements of it are present. Although the Soviet Union could not possibly become so dominant as to exclude the United States from the region, the Soviet Union's ability to project military power through its expanding naval presence in the Pacific and its close association with Vietnam, which has the largest military force in the region, is a matter of some concern.[11] As is often noted, ASEAN countries sit astride some of the world's busiest shipping lanes, like the Strait of Malacca. Restricted access would have serious economic and strategic implications for the United States and Japan. Of course the principal guarantee of continued access is good relations with ASEAN governments; however, the ability to counter any Soviet threat is important.

The United States maintains military bases in the Philippines and has a mutual defense treaty and a mutual assistance agreement with the Philippines. Thus the United States does have enough military capability in the region to play its explicit (for the Philippines and Thailand) and implicit (for the others) role as guarantor against an external threat to ASEAN from a potential hostile power. The willingness of the United States to continue in this role was questioned after the Vietnam War, when some feared the United States might totally withdraw from Southeast Asia. Even though that fear was countered by efforts of the Carter administration, in particular by the renewing of the base agreement with the Philip-

11. Use of port facilities in Vietnam essentially doubles the on-station sea time of the Soviet fleet operating in the region.

pines in January 1979, some lingering ambiguity exists about the extent of the U.S. commitment.

Although not very likely, a big-power conflict in the region could grow out of Sino-Soviet rivalry, with Vietnam acting as a catalyst. Such a conflict might spill over into ASEAN countries (especially Thailand) despite their earnest efforts not to take sides. It is just such an eventuality that legitimizes U.S. military presence in the region for some of the ASEAN countries.[12]

The United States has a political and ideological interest in ASEAN countries because all the governments are friendly to it and committed to rapid economic growth through private initiative, with private enterprises playing the major developmental role. Since the views of the ASEAN countries on how to manage their economies are so compatible with American views, their economic success is of great symbolic as well as economic interest to the United States. In the case of the Philippines, however, U.S. interest goes much further. The history of colonial and commonwealth ties, the comradeship in arms in the war against Japan, the explicit security connection, and the existence of a large Filipino immigrant community in the United States create what is properly described as a special relationship. According to Robert Pringle, the legacy of U.S. involvement with the Philippines "included faith in the possibility of upward economic mobility, heightened respect for the accumulation of wealth, and the enshrinement of democratic political forms, if not democratic substance."[13]

Unfortunately, their long association does not mean that the United States understands the nuances of its current relationship with the Philippines, nor is American understanding of current reality in other ASEAN countries very profound. To describe these countries as being in a post-colonial era ignores the great importance of their recent history. These are mature countries with sophisticated political systems. This is not to suggest that political change cannot take place. Since all the ASEAN countries have been sustaining rapid economic growth and economic growth is itself a fundamental cause of political change, political change is to be expected. However, these changes will grow out of their indigenous experiences and will not be determined from the outside.

Failure to appreciate this point can lead to two different kinds of errors in U.S. policy. It can lead to aggressive and interventionist efforts to mold

12. Robert Pringle, *Indonesia and the Philippines: American Interests in Island Southeast Asia* (Columbia University Press, 1980), chap. 3.

13. Ibid., p. 10.

these societies in ways Americans think desirable, without recognizing that they cannot be manipulated from abroad.[14] Or it can lead to an indecisive position that fails to promote U.S. interest sufficiently to meet the Japanese challenge. It is wrong to believe that these societies are fragile and unable to provide the countervailing power needed for a good, long-term working relationship with the United States. On the contrary, the ASEAN countries have been tested and have met internal and external stress. They can adequately defend themselves in meeting vigorous efforts by the United States to promote its own legitimate interests.

Japanese Policies

Since emerging as an economic superpower in the early 1970s, Japan has given special attention to its bilateral relations with ASEAN countries and has taken ASEAN as an institution very seriously. The roots of this interest may derive from Japan's wartime experience and its postwar reparations arrangements with each of the countries. Six Japanese prime ministers have taken steps to strengthen Japan's ties to these countries.

The reasons for this attention are many and varied. Japan's economic interest is substantial and rising. Japan is constantly seeking new markets for its exports, and the rapid growth of ASEAN countries has attracted many Japanese firms. Recent episodes involving Japanese exports of automobiles suggest that protectionism may be increasing in Europe and North America, and it may be aimed particularly at Japanese firms. Consequently, pressure to find markets elsewhere has grown. Moreover, Japan is now seeking new sources of raw material imports, which ASEAN countries can supply. That ASEAN countries are willing to permit foreign firms to have equity participation in their natural resource development also serves Japan's desire to enlarge its foreign investment. After the 1973–74 disruption of the petroleum market by the Organization of Petroleum Exporting Countries (OPEC), and the ensuing threat of resource nationalism affecting other raw materials, Japan's interest in doing business with the pragmatic ASEAN countries increased all the more. The essence of Japan's strategy in dealing with resource security problems is diversification so as to minimize risks, and ASEAN countries fit well within this strategy, even though they are not large enough to solve all Japan's problems.

14. This misconception is perpetuated in part by Filipino immigrants who try to influence American policy toward the Philippines for their own partisan purposes.

Japan has important military security interest in ASEAN countries as well. As already noted, ASEAN countries sit astride crucial shipping lanes to Japan, but that is only part of Japan's concern. Continued instability in Indochina is threatening to Japan, particularly because it could bring about another war in Asia. ASEAN is viewed as a stabilizing force in Southeast Asia, and thus it benefits Japan.

Japan regards ASEAN countries as offering many opportunities for a more active foreign policy. Because some ASEAN countries perceive the Soviet Union as the main threat to the region while others put China in that role, and because the United States lost prestige owing to the Vietnam War and years of economic difficulties, Japan feels it has much room to maneuver to improve its own position in the region.[15] It therefore believes it has an advantage over the other major powers contesting for influence in ASEAN.

But Japan has many difficulties to overcome in promoting its diplomacy. First, the memories of World War II are still vivid, especially in the Philippines. Consequently, Japan cannot offer military cooperation as an inducement to closer relations. It must limit the projection of its naval forces into ASEAN waters and minimize the perception of the military power it does possess so as not to create unease among its southern neighbors.

Second, Japan's diplomacy suffers from the fact that Japan is so large and economically powerful relative to individual countries, or even to ASEAN countries as a group. Japan dominates ASEAN trade and investment, which stirs up resentment and raises charges of overpresence. Though of overwhelming importance to member countries, ASEAN is considered of only modest importance to Japan. For instance, Japan buys most of ASEAN commodity exports, but ASEAN countries provide only a small share of Japan's total imports of these commodities. Furthermore, Japan usually runs trade surpluses with these countries, which invites their charges that it is buying too little from them. They point mainly to Japan's trade barriers as the cause of the unbalance. And indeed Japan's tariff structure escalates according to the stage of production, with raw materials generally given duty-free status while processed materials face a stiff fee. For example, the sale of logs and wood chips to Japan is promoted, but the

15. Turo Yano, "ASEAN in the New Setting of Asia: A Japanese View," Presentation in Sarasin Viraphol, Amphon Namatra, and Masahide Shibusawa, eds., *The ASEAN: Problems and Prospects in a Changing World*, Proceedings of a Conference held December 18–20, 1975, at Chulalongkorn University, Bangkok, Thailand (Tokyo: East-West Seminar, and Bangkok: Chulalongkorn University, Institute of Asian Studies, 1976), pp. 207–12.

importation of higher-valued lumber, plywood, furniture, and paper is limited.

Finally, Japan's own diplomatic style at times hinders its relations with ASEAN countries. The slow and difficult process of building a consensus in Tokyo means that Japan often reacts too late to diplomatic opportunities. Also, its unwillingness to step forward with proposals to solve problems opens it to charges of avoiding responsibility. As an example, the main ASEAN security concern at present is the occupation of Kampuchea by Vietnam. Yet Japan refuses to suggest any ways that Vietnamese troops might be dislodged, and some diplomats from ASEAN countries resent this lack of leadership.

For many years Japan stressed its bilateral relations with individual ASEAN countries. Shortly after the formation of ASEAN in 1967, Prime Minister Eisaku Sato visited all five countries, but it was more of a fact-finding inspection tour than part of a comprehensive foreign policy.[16] Most Japanese interest at this time was focused on resource-rich Indonesia and Thailand. But soon Japanese business became very active in both trade and investment in the area, creating many of the problems previously noted. The strained relations between these countries and Japan were reflected in the move by Thailand in 1972 to boycott Japanese goods. And in January 1974, when the first oil crisis had increased Japan's concern over natural resource security, Prime Minister Kakuei Tanaka made his well-remembered trip to the ASEAN countries. It was hoped that his visit would moderate anti-Japanese feelings, but instead it touched off civil disturbances in both Indonesia and Thailand. Although the roots of the disturbances may have been more closely linked to discontent with their own governments than with Japan, rioters vented their anger against visible signs of Japanese encroachment. The Tanaka trip marked one of the low points of Japan's postwar relations with the region.

Japan responded to the challenge by rethinking its policy. In the summer of 1975 Prime Minister Takeo Miki sent Saburo Okita, then head of Japan's aid agency (the Overseas Economic Cooperation Fund), to the ASEAN countries to survey the situation. By then Saigon had fallen, and political leaders were seriously worried about Vietnam. Okita encountered scarcely any criticism of Japan; instead he found that the ASEAN countries wanted greater economic cooperation with it.[17] And even though

16. Makoto Ikema, "Japan's Economic Relations with ASEAN," in Garnaut, ed., *ASEAN in a Changing Pacific and World Economy*, pp. 453–80.

17. Saburo Okita, "ASEAN and Its Relations with Japan and the United States," in

Prime Minister Miki was not invited to the first ASEAN summit meeting in 1976, his expressed interest in attending it was taken as a positive sign of Japan's concern.

The visit by Prime Minister Takeo Fukuda in July 1977 marked the beginning of Japan's active diplomacy toward ASEAN. In Kuala Lumpur he announced that Japan would favorably consider contributing $1 billion to the five ASEAN industrial projects, would cooperate in establishing a commodity stabilization scheme (like the European Community's STABEX for its associated countries), would help ASEAN countries increase their exports to Japan, and would provide financial support for cultural exchanges between ASEAN countries and Japan. In Manila he proclaimed the so-called Fukuda doctrine, defining Japan's relations with the ASEAN countries. Three principles were enunciated: that Japan is an economic and not a military power; that Japan intends to expand social, political, and cultural ties along with economic ones; and that Japan desires the establishment of a relationship based on mutual understanding.[18]

When Masayoshi Ohira became prime minister at the end of 1978, a new pan-Pacific diplomacy was inaugurated in recognition of the dawning of the "Pacific Age."[19] It was recognized that the ASEAN-Japan relationship was among the most important in Southeast Asia. Japan's foreign minister became a regular participant in joint meetings of foreign ministers after the annual ASEAN foreign ministers conference; thus bilateral meetings between Japan and ASEAN became institutionalized. While the untimely death of Ohira has apparently put Japan's foreign policy initiative for the Pacific on hold, Prime Minister Zenko Suzuki has followed the new tradition of making a comprehensive trip to ASEAN countries. The symbolic importance of making this trip before making his first official visit to Washington was not lost on the ASEAN countries. And during the trip Prime Minister Suzuki indicated that Japan is committed to a long-term program of aid to them.[20]

Japan's economic cooperation with ASEAN, however, has been less enthusiastic than Fukuda's 1977 plans might suggest. Little if any of the $1

Leon Hollerman, ed., *Japan and the United States: Economic and Political Adversaries* (Westview Press, 1980), pp. 97–110.

18. Seiji Naya, "Japan's Role in ASEAN Economic Development" (University of Hawaii, n.d.), p. 5.

19. Saburo Okita, *The Developing Economies and Japan* (University of Tokyo Press, 1980), p. 268.

20. Yasuhiko Nara, "Japan's Growing Foreign Aid," *Wall Street Journal*, March 23, 1981.

billion Japanese contribution to ASEAN industrial projects has been spent, though that has probably more to do with the inherent problems of those projects, as discussed in chapter 2, than to Japanese reluctance. The Japanese did study a possible STABEX scheme for ASEAN called ASEBEX.[21] The costs to Japan would have been a relatively modest $100 million annually plus an original investment of about $160 million, but Japan refused to move forward on the proposal despite continued ASEAN interest. However, Japan does provide a growing amount of aid to ASEAN countries. In 1979, 29.8 percent of Japanese bilateral official development assistance, amounting to $572 million, went to these countries, principally to Indonesia.[22] The amount of other Japanese aid has also been increasing. ASEAN permits Japan to rationalize the regional balance of its aid and overseas investment in that ASEAN makes all the member countries attractive to Japan, not just one or two of them.[23] Furthermore, with government encouragement, Japanese business has formed the ASEAN-Japan Development Corporation to promote Japanese investment.[24]

Japan, the United States, and ASEAN

Japan recognizes that it has both a complementary and a competitive relationship with the United States in affairs pertaining to ASEAN. Japan and the United States fully agree on the need for stability, security, and prosperity in the region, and to this end they both desire ASEAN to flourish. Thus they have a basis for cooperative policy to strengthen ASEAN. But there is a limit to how far U.S.-Japanese cooperation can be pushed before it causes problems in ASEAN countries. The ASEAN countries are fearful of being dominated by the rich countries of the Pacific and will view skeptically joint U.S.-Japanese efforts on their behalf. They want Japan to compete with the United States for their favor for obvious and understandable reasons. Therefore, combined U.S.-Japanese initiatives must be circumscribed.

21. The International Development Center of Japan carried out an econometric study with a group of experts from Southeast Asia and Japan. See Okita, *Developing Economies and Japan*, pp. 266–67.

22. Japan External Trade Organization, *Economic Cooperation of Japan, 1980* (Tokyo: JETRO, 1981), tables 12, 27, 37, 42, 53.

23. Miyohei Shinohara, "Japan's Strategies towards New Developments in the Economies of East and Southeast Asia," *Contemporary Southeast Asia*, vol. 1 (May 1979), pp. 75–91.

24. *ASEAN Briefing*, no. 36 (July 1981) (published in Hong Kong by Asia Letter Ltd).

Moreover, Japan may see its relations with ASEAN countries as a way to offset some of its losses should the United States succeed in making economic inroads into China. Japan had a major share of the Chinese market (though that position has been achieved not without difficulties and reverses). Now that the United States is contesting for markets on the mainland, Japan can use the improving Chinese-U.S. relationship as an argument to weaken resentment of Japan in ASEAN countries, since they, like Taiwan, fear the implications of the evolving Chinese economic relations with market-oriented economies.

More directly, however, Japanese firms see themselves in competition with U.S. business in ASEAN countries. Japanese firms want to maintain their position in the region, and American firms are the only major commercial threat to them. The essence of a successful diversification strategy is to increase one's alternative markets and sources while reducing those of trading partners. To the degree that Japanese firms can demonstrate that ASEAN countries have no alternatives to heavy dependence on Japan, the more secure that position becomes. Consequently, American firms and European firms have some advantages in competing for business in the region because the ASEAN countries understand this Japanese strategy and want to sustain economic ties to other countries.

Chapter Four

U.S. Merchandise Trade with ASEAN

The economies of the ASEAN countries are much more open to international influences than those of most other developing countries, and the economy of Singapore is freer of restrictions than any economy. As a result, the ASEAN countries are increasing their interactions with the entire world, but particularly with other countries in the Pacific basin.[1]

The most important kind of international interaction for the ASEAN countries is international trade of merchandise. Most of the economic gains that are expected to arise from ASEAN membership relate to the trade of goods, which is examined in this chapter. Of growing importance, however, is the international trade of services, ranging from engineering services to insurance and tourism. Furthermore, direct investment in ASEAN countries by foreign firms is important in industry, commerce, and finance. Capital flows other than direct investment are also significant for some of the countries. And for many countries, migration of people is of political, strategic, and military concern as well as of economic importance. Some of these economic flows are examined in chapter 5.

The external orientation of the ASEAN countries has significant implications for U.S. economic performance and international economic policy. It is in the ASEAN market that the U.S. ability to compete with Japan will be given its purest test. Indeed, U.S. economic relations with Japan will be affected by the performance of the U.S. and Japanese economies in ASEAN. Furthermore, U.S. policies have a strong influence on the ASEAN economies regardless of whether they are intended to or not. Most U.S. policies that affect ASEAN were drawn or legislated without ASEAN in mind. Thus the results of policy for good or ill have been accidental or idiosyncratic. This chapter examines the dimensions of U.S. merchandise trade with ASEAN countries compared with those of Japan in order to discover the causes of U.S. export successes and failures in preparation for the policy discussion in the last two chapters.

1. Lawrence B. Krause and Sueo Sekiguchi, *Economic Interaction in the Pacific Basin* (Brookings Institution, 1980), chap. 1.

The Big Picture

In 1979 the United States exported $6.8 billion in merchandise to the ASEAN countries and imported $10.0 billion from them.[2] This represented just 3.7 percent of total U.S. exports and 4.6 percent of U.S. imports in that year. But since U.S. exports to ASEAN were only about $1 billion as recently as 1970, they had grown at an annual rate of 22.4 percent during the 1970s. In the same period total U.S. exports grew 17.3 percent a year. Similarly, U.S. imports from ASEAN grew 26.8 percent a year, while total U.S. imports advanced only 20.0 percent. Hence ASEAN expanded its share of both U.S. exports and imports.

It is interesting to compare U.S. experience with Japan's. Japanese exports of merchandise to ASEAN amounted to $9.6 billion in 1979, having grown at a 20.3 percent annual rate during the 1970s. This growth rate, however, was no greater than that of total Japanese exports; thus the ASEAN share of Japanese exports, 9.4 percent, did not change during the decade. Japanese imports from ASEAN were $16.1 billion in 1979, having grown 27.1 percent a year during the 1970s, while total Japanese imports increased 21.6 percent a year. So ASEAN countries became a more important supplier of merchandise to Japan but not a more important market for its goods.

Because of the rapid expansion of ASEAN total merchandise trade, neither the U.S. nor the Japanese experience appears unusual from the perspective of ASEAN countries. The United States just about managed to hold its share of ASEAN imports, which was 14.8 percent in 1970 and 14.6 percent in 1979, but Japan's share declined from 24.5 percent in 1970 to 20.6 percent in 1979. The two countries did become more important markets for ASEAN goods, but only marginally. The U.S. share rose from 19.3 to 19.7 percent and Japan's from 30.6 to 31.8 percent. Thus in 1979 the United States and Japan together provided 35.4 percent of ASEAN imports and purchased 51.5 percent of ASEAN exports.

Because of the difference in the size of the economies, the United States is more important to ASEAN than ASEAN is to the United States; however, ASEAN's rapid economic growth is gradually changing the balance. For the 1970s it would appear that the United States was able to meet the competition of Japan, ASEAN's most important trading partner.

2. The data in this section are from the International Monetary Fund, Direction of Trade tapes, which provide annual data on aggregate exports and imports for IMF member countries. Percentage changes and shares of trade were calculated from these figures.

A bit more insight is obtained by examining U.S. export performance in the individual ASEAN countries. In 1970 over one-third of U.S. exports to ASEAN went to the Philippines, 24 percent to Indonesia, 22 percent to Singapore, 14 percent to Thailand, and 6 percent to Malaysia. During the 1970s the total imports of Indonesia and Singapore grew 24.5 percent a year and those of the other three ASEAN countries 21 percent a year. U.S. exports did well in Singapore, where the U.S. share rose from 10.8 percent of the market in 1970 to 14.4 percent in 1979. U.S. exports also did well in Malaysia, rising from 8.6 percent of the market in 1970 to 15.1 percent in 1979. The U.S. share of Thailand's imports rose somewhat, from 14.8 to 16.6 percent. But in the fast-growing Indonesian market, the U.S. share dropped from 17.8 to 14.6 percent, and in the Philippines from 29.4 to 23.0 percent. Therefore, the U.S. export success was primarily due to good performance in Singapore and Malaysia, which offset relatively poor performance in Indonesia and the Philippines.

The United States has been losing shares of total world export markets for much of the last quarter-century. In earlier years this was neither surprising nor particularly worrisome. It reflected the recovery of other industrial countries from the disruptions of war and their embarkment on rapid economic growth, and occurred when the U.S. economy was performing very well by its own historical standard. But during the last ten years or so, the U.S. economy has not performed well. Productivity growth has slowed and inflation has risen. The U.S. balance of trade has shifted from surplus to deficit, and in many years the United States has been forced into foreign borrowing to cover a current account deficit in its balance of payments. Under these circumstances the continued erosion of U.S. shares of world markets is disturbing: it reflects shortcomings of the United States, not just success of others. Consequently, the good performance of U.S. exports in ASEAN markets is particularly important, since it suggests that a decline of U.S. market shares is not inevitable.

The erosion of the U.S. position in world trade has been documented in many studies. An extensive study by the government, published in 1980, pointed out that the erosion of market shares since 1962 was moderated by U.S. success in exporting high-technology products, capital equipment (an overlapping category with high technology), and agricultural products.[3] In these product areas the United States earned increasing trade surpluses.

3. U.S. Department of Labor, Office of Foreign Economic Research, *Report of the President on U.S. Competitiveness, Together with the Study on U.S. Competitiveness* (Government Printing Office, 1980).

The study noted, however, that the U.S. lead in high-technology products during the 1970s was narrowed considerably, especially by West Germany and Japan. Indeed, Japan has joined the United States in having a competitive advantage in a number of high-technology products. Hence examination of the competitive struggle between American and Japanese firms to export high-technology products to ASEAN countries is of great interest.

Commodity Structure of U.S.-ASEAN Trade

Further insight into U.S. trade relations with ASEAN countries comes from examining the commodity structure of imports and exports by major subgroups.[4] At the start of the 1970s (average of 1970 and 1971), about two-thirds of U.S. imports from ASEAN were raw materials, mainly food and crude materials (other than fuels). For example, ASEAN countries supplied 56.3 percent of total U.S. imports of animal and vegetable oils and fats. Moreover, semifinished manufactures constituted a large part of the one-third of U.S. imports from ASEAN countries that were manufactures.

By the end of the decade (average of 1978 and 1979), the structure of U.S. imports from ASEAN countries had shifted considerably. The largest single item was mineral fuels (38 percent of total imports from ASEAN), reflecting the rise of fuel prices and the fact that the United States was then getting about 7 percent of its petroleum import needs from ASEAN countries, compared with only 2 percent earlier. Furthermore, manufactured goods became more important (38 percent of total U.S. imports from ASEAN), led by the growth of machinery, transport, and other equipment, and such manufactures as textiles, clothing, and footwear. For many categories of manufactures, ASEAN countries were providing about 3 percent of U.S. imports by the end of the decade, as opposed to about 1 percent at its start. ASEAN, however, still dominated U.S. imports of animal and vegetable oils, supplying over 70 percent of the total. The United States is itself a large producer and exporter of animal and vegetable oils, and ASEAN countries were the only real competitors for the strong U.S. position in world markets.

By contrast, over 90 percent of Japanese imports from ASEAN countries, both at the beginning and at the end of the 1970s, were food and raw materials, although mineral fuels increased in importance during the de-

4. The data in this section come from UN Commodity Trade tapes, which provide information on specific disaggregated commodity trade between nations.

cade as they did for the United States. Japanese imports of manufactures from ASEAN countries grew, but largely in the semifinished category.

The structure of U.S. exports to ASEAN countries at the beginning of the 1970s was about 75 percent manufactured goods; by the end of the decade it was over 80 percent. In both periods machinery and transport equipment made up about half of U.S. exports to ASEAN, and the ASEAN market became slightly more important, rising from 3 to 4 percent of total U.S. exports of that type. Of note was the importance of chemicals, which grew from 7.4 to 23.3 percent of U.S. exports to ASEAN, while the ASEAN market advanced from 2 to 8 percent of total U.S. exports of chemicals. U.S. agricultural products continued to find a market in ASEAN countries, although their share of total U.S. exports to ASEAN countries declined from 13 to 9 percent.

As one would expect, Japanese exports to ASEAN countries are almost exclusively manufactured goods. In the early 1970s, 40 percent of Japanese exports to ASEAN were semifinished manufactures, 40 percent machinery and transport equipment, 10 percent chemicals, and about 10 percent other manufactures and primary products. By the end of the decade, over half of Japanese exports were machinery and transport equipment; however, the ASEAN market remained at about 8 percent of total Japanese exports of this type. In the later period semifinished manufactures had dropped to less than 30 percent of Japanese exports to ASEAN while chemicals remained at 10 percent. It is significant, however, that the ASEAN market became more important for Japanese exports of chemicals, reaching 15 percent of their total exports, which was not true of other types of manufactures.

The differences between U.S. and Japanese success in various product groups in the ASEAN market during the 1970s are seen in ratios of the exports of the two countries to this market. In the early 1970s U.S. exports of chemicals were less than 50 percent of those from Japan, but by the end of the decade they were more than 50 percent larger. On the other hand, U.S. exports of machinery and transport equipment and miscellaneous manufactured goods were 72 percent and 63 percent, respectively, of Japanese exports at the beginning of the period, but dropped to 63 percent and 49 percent, respectively, at its end.

Factor Characteristics of U.S.-ASEAN Trade

Why did the United States have more success than Japan with some U.S. exports to ASEAN countries, such as chemicals, and less success with others? And why were U.S. exporters able to win a larger share of the market of some ASEAN countries but not of others? The reasons for the success or failure of different U.S. manufactured products in international trade have been examined by Aho, Bowen, and Pelzman.[5] Because the authors used varying definitions of success and failure for different products, their results were not entirely consistent. Nevertheless, some of their findings were clear. They determined that American export success was found in products in which research and development expenditures as a share of value added in production were relatively high, in products in which scientists and engineers as a percent of total employment were high, and in products in which professional and technical workers as a percent of total employment were high. These are attributes of high-technology products and possibly of human capital–intensive ones. On the other hand, U.S. trade failures were in products requiring a relatively large amount of capital per worker and in those requiring a relatively large number of production workers as a percent of total employment. Thus it would appear that insight into U.S. trade performance can be obtained by examining some characteristics of different commodities, especially the factors involved in their production.

In recent years many economists have worked on amending the theory of international trade to reflect a changing world economy and on testing their ideas empirically.[6] While no single theory appears adequate to explain the trade of all countries at all times, some general approaches are now widely accepted as supplements to the classical theory of comparative advantage. In my work commodities are considered to result from five factor inputs: natural resources, unskilled labor, physical capital, human capital (skilled labor), and technology.[7]

5. Michael Aho, Harry P. Bowen, and Joseph Pelzman, "Assessing the Changing Structure of U.S. Trade in Manufactured Goods: An Analysis and Comparison of Various Indicators of Comparative Advantage and Competitiveness," July 1980, in the appendix to *Report of the President on U.S. Competitiveness.*

6. Two useful reviews of the literature are William H. Branson, "Trends in United States International Trade and Comparative Advantage: Analysis and Prospects," in National Science Foundation, *International Economic Policy Research*, Papers and Proceedings of a Colloquium held in Washington, D.C., October 3–4, 1980 (NSF, 1980), sec. 3, pp. 22–48; and Robert M. Stern, "Changes in U.S. Comparative Advantage: Issues for Research and Policy," in ibid., sec. 3, pp. 81–105.

7. This is not to suggest that production can take place without entrepreneurship. Indeed, a particular form of entrepreneurship, multinational firms, has received much attention in the literature. However, since entrepreneurship is required for all production, it does not differentiate among products. In the formulation here, the special role of multinational corporations is subsumed under the factor of technology.

Most products require inputs of all five factors, and therefore factor inputs occur in combination. Nevertheless, products can be classified according to their dominant factor, the one that is generally used most intensively in production and that largely determines the location of production. Particular stress is put on the location-specific character of factors. A factor of production that is readily transferred between countries is not likely to be the major determinant of where a good is produced.

For this study each of the 105 products that comprise U.S. exports has been put into one of four factor groups: natural resource intensive, labor intensive, technology intensive, and human capital intensive.[8] The products easiest to classify are those that require significant inputs of natural resources, since existence of the natural resource is a necessary condition for production. Thus any product requiring a large amount of natural resources has been classified as natural resource intensive even if it also requires large amounts of other resources like physical capital and unskilled labor. Production of such goods is expected to occur where the appropriate natural resource is found in relative abundance.

Products classified as labor intensive are those in which unskilled labor constitutes the main ingredient in value added in production. The production process of labor-intensive goods, such as clothing and shoes, involves well-known, widely dispersed, and relatively unchanging technology that is often embodied in machinery that itself moves easily in international trade. Even though unskilled labor does move between countries, the amount of immigration is small relative to total labor force (except in rare cases). Therefore, production of labor-intensive goods is expected to occur in countries where unskilled labor is relatively abundant.

Technology-intensive goods, such as computers and airplanes, are produced in industries that expend a significant amount of resources in research and development, as measured by the share of R&D in value added in production. Since R&D involves both new products and new processes, the relevant industries change over time. However, there is comparatively little change within a single decade. The production of technology-intensive goods is expected to take place primarily in the country where R&D expenditures occur. Technology is transferable internationally, frequently within the confines of the same firm, so the location of production is not uniquely

8. See the appendix for a description of the classification procedure and for the complete list of export products. The number of these products depends on the classification system being used, and no significance should be attached to it.

determined. Nevertheless, the tendency to produce where the R&D occurs is still strong.

Human capital–intensive products are those that require a significant amount of skilled labor; that is, labor whose skills are obtained by investment in human capital. Such products are difficult to identify and locate in production because human capital is hard to measure and is often combined with technology and physical capital, and because skilled labor is transferable internationally. Nevertheless, studies by Branson and Monoyios and confirmed by Stern and Maskus indicate that human capital intensity is a major factor characterizing U.S. exports and therefore must be separately identified.[9] The production of human capital–intensive products is expected to take place primarily where there is heavy investment in human capital both by the educational system and by educational training on the job through formal or informal work training programs.

For several reasons physical capital was not used as a factor for classification purposes. First, it is always combined with other factors in the production of any good. And second, it is the factor most easily transferred internationally and so provides the least guidance to the location of production. The fact that capital is mobile does not imply that the capital intensity of production is the same regardless of location. For example, copper will be mined through a more capital-intensive method in the United States than in the Philippines because wages are lower in the Philippines. However, in both countries copper is mined because of the presence of copper deposits, not because of the local availability of capital.

A Comparison of Japanese and American Trade

This section examines the factor characteristics of U.S. and Japanese exports to the ASEAN countries and the world, as well as the characteristics of ASEAN imports. The following section deals specifically with the export of high-technology products.

U.S. Exports to ASEAN and the World

As seen in table 4-1, total U.S. exports during the 1970s showed considerable stability in factor characteristics. The largest category of U.S. ex-

9. William H. Branson and Nikolaos Monoyios, "Factor Inputs in U.S. Trade," *Journal of International Economics*, vol. 7 (May 1977); and Robert M. Stern and Keith E. Maskus, "Determinants of the Structure of U.S. Foreign Trade, 1958–76," *Journal of International Economics*, vol. 11 (May 1981), pp. 207–24.

Table 4-1. *Factor Characteristics of U.S. Exports to ASEAN and to the World, 1970-79*
Percent

Place and year	Natural resource intensive	Technology intensive	Labor intensive	Human capital intensive
ASEAN				
1970	30.8	46.3	5.1	17.9
1971	27.1	50.2	4.4	18.2
1972	28.4	53.4	3.9	14.3
1973	26.5	55.7	4.1	13.7
1974	18.4	63.3	3.6	14.8
1975	16.2	65.8	3.1	14.9
1976	19.0	64.9	3.2	12.9
1977	21.2	63.5	3.8	11.4
1978	22.0	64.0	3.1	11.0
1979	17.4	71.2	2.3	9.1
World				
1970	31.3	45.1	4.0	19.6
1971	29.2	46.3	4.2	20.3
1972	30.6	44.5	4.6	20.3
1973	36.7	40.8	4.3	18.2
1974	34.7	41.9	4.5	18.9
1975	32.3	44.1	3.9	19.7
1976	31.3	44.5	4.5	19.6
1977	31.1	44.6	4.5	19.8
1978	31.6	45.4	4.4	18.6
1979	32.6	45.5	4.6	17.3

Source: UN Commodity Trade tapes. Figures are rounded.

ports was technology-intensive products, which made up about 45 percent of the total. Second was natural resource–intensive products, at about 32 percent. Human capital–intensive products made up 19 percent and labor-intensive products just 4 percent.[10] Over the decade natural resource–intensive and labor-intensive products became only slightly more important and human capital–intensive products only slightly less.

In contrast, U.S. exports to ASEAN countries during the 1970s showed distinct changes. Technology increasingly became the dominant force be-

10. Human capital is less significant in this classification than in some earlier systems because technology is separately identified, and the two variables tend to overlap. Stern and Maskus "Determinants of the Structure of U.S. Foreign Trade," found that human capital did not improve the statistical explanation once technology had been introduced as an explanatory variable.

hind these exports: products in that category rose from 46 percent of exports in 1970 to over 70 percent in 1979. All other categories declined, including natural resources from 31 to 17 percent, human capital from 18 to 9 percent, and unskilled labor from 5 to 2 percent. The message from these data seems clear. The success the United States has achieved in exporting to the rapidly expanding ASEAN markets has been due to the competitiveness of its technology.

Several influences have contributed to this observed trend. Advanced industrial countries are already much alike in levels of income and technology. The gains from international trade among these countries are more likely to arise from economies of scale brought about by specialization within particular industries than from divergent factor endowments. Much of this trade is therefore intraindustry trade, characterized by broadly similar factor inputs that show little change over time even though total trade is growing. Trade between industrial countries and developing countries—even advanced developing countries—is usually quite different. Their levels of income and technology are likely to be dissimilar, and their different factor endowments are likely to be the source of gains from trade. Interindustry trade is generally dominant. Within manufacturing, the industrial countries are likely to be exporting technology-intensive and human capital–intensive products to the developing countries and importing labor-intensive products from them. The faster the economic growth of the developing countries, the larger will be the share of investment goods in their economies and the greater will be the share of technology-intensive goods in their imports.

Technology-intensive exports also appear to be the source of the differences in U.S. export success in the various ASEAN countries. As noted earlier, U.S. exports during the 1970s did particularly well in Singapore and Malaysia, moderately well in Thailand, and relatively badly in Indonesia and the Philippines. The technology share of U.S. exports to each of the ASEAN countries is shown in figure 4-1. The line for ASEAN as a whole shows the pattern noted in table 4-1 (plotted as a two-year moving average). The technology share rose in the first half of the decade, stabilized in the middle, and rose again at the end. In the two successful markets for U.S. exports, Singapore and Malaysia, the technology share was high at the start of the 1970s and rose throughout the decade. In Thailand the technology share was relatively low at the beginning of the 1970s but rose moderately later. The technology share in both the Philippines and Indonesia, however, followed a different pattern. It was low at the start of the

Figure 4-1. *Percent Share of Technology-Intensive Products in Total U.S.*
Exports to ASEAN Countries, 1970-79

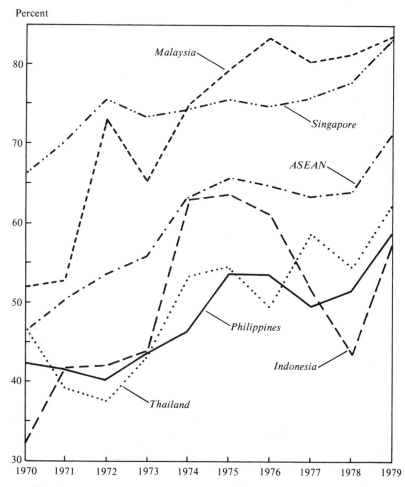

Percent

Source: UN Commodity Trade tapes. Percentages are a two-year moving average.

decade, rose in the middle years, and declined at the end of the 1970s,
especially in Indonesia. Thus the lack of success of American exporters of
technology products to Indonesia and the Philippines after 1974–75 appears to be the source of U.S. export disappointments and, as will be shown
subsequently, did not occur because of the pattern of demand in those
countries.

Table 4-2. *Factor Characteristics of Japanese Exports to ASEAN and to the World, 1970–79*

Percent

Place and year	Natural resource intensive	Technology intensive	Labor intensive	Human capital intensive
ASEAN				
1970	8.8	34.3	17.1	39.7
1971	9.0	34.5	16.8	39.7
1972	7.7	35.1	19.6	37.7
1973	8.1	34.7	16.4	40.8
1974	7.7	36.2	13.0	43.1
1975	6.4	35.0	16.7	41.9
1976	6.8	36.9	15.1	41.2
1977	6.9	37.3	11.2	44.6
World				
1970	8.4	25.4	24.0	42.3
1971	7.5	24.4	22.8	45.3
1972	6.9	25.9	21.7	45.4
1973	6.7	26.9	21.4	45.0
1974	7.5	26.4	18.7	47.5
1975	5.8	28.0	18.8	47.3
1976	5.2	27.9	18.5	48.4
1977	4.9	29.1	17.9	48.1
1978	4.8	32.1	14.1	49.0
1979	5.2	33.6	10.3	51.0

Source: UN Commodity Trade tapes. Figures are rounded.

Japanese Exports to ASEAN and the World

Japanese exports were also classified under the same system. The results are shown in table 4-2. Human capital–intensive products make up the largest share of Japanese exports to world markets. At the beginning of the 1970s, they amounted to 42 percent of the total and increased to 51 percent by 1979. The share of technology-intensive products also rose from 25 percent at the start to 34 percent at the end of the decade. The shares of labor-intensive and natural resource–intensive products fell, going from 24 to 10 percent and from 8 to 5 percent, respectively.

The distribution of Japanese exports to ASEAN countries was quite similar to its global pattern—and even more so at the end of the decade than at the beginning. The shares of human capital products and technology products rose and the shares of unskilled labor and natural resource products fell, but in all cases the changes were less marked than in Japan's exports to the world as a whole.

Furthermore, the pattern of Japan's exports to each of the ASEAN countries is essentially the same. For example, during the 1970s the share of technology-intensive products in Japan's exports increased by 3 percentage points to Thailand, 5 percentage points to the Philippines, 6 percentage points to Indonesia, 7 percentage points to Malaysia, and 13 percentage points to Singapore. But the Singapore share rose so much only because it was out of line with the shares of the other countries in 1970. In 1979 the technology share in Japanese exports was 41 percent to both the Philippines and Indonesia; 42 percent to both Thailand and Malaysia, and 43 percent to Singapore.

If there were any peculiarities in the ASEAN market or in member countries individually, they apparently did not influence Japanese exports to those markets. The pattern of Japan's comparative advantage that has been established in world markets was duplicated in ASEAN countries.

ASEAN Imports from the United States and Japan

Further insight is obtained by shifting the focus to ASEAN imports, in particular those from the United States and Japan (table 4-3).[11] ASEAN imports from all sources at the start of the 1970s were made up of 34 percent natural resource–intensive products, 32 percent technology-intensive products, 24 percent human capital–intensive products, and 11 percent labor-intensive products. By 1977 natural resource products had risen to 41 percent, technology products had declined slightly to 31 percent, human capital products had declined to 21 percent, and unskilled labor products had declined to 7 percent. Given this ASEAN pattern, the U.S. structure of exports at the start of the decade was better positioned than that of Japan to benefit from the growth of demand during the 1970s, although neither country could benefit from the rise of ASEAN petroleum imports. U.S. exports were concentrated in high-technology products and to a lesser extent natural resource products, whereas Japanese exports were concentrated in human capital products along with high-technology and unskilled labor products. From this perspective, therefore, it is not surprising that U.S. exports to ASEAN rose rapidly, or even that during several years the

11. The data reported by ASEAN are not available beyond 1977 and are therefore less complete than the data reported by the United States and Japan.

Table 4-3. *ASEAN Imports from the World, and Shares Provided by the United States and Japan, by Factor Characteristics, 1971–77*
Percent

Place and year	Natural resource intensive	Technology intensive	Labor intensive	Human capital intensive
World				
1971	34.0	31.9	10.5	23.6
1972	32.9	33.9	10.1	23.0
1973	32.6	33.9	9.9	23.7
1974	37.1	33.6	7.3	22.0
1975	36.7	35.2	6.7	21.6
1976	39.6	32.9	7.4	20.1
1977	41.0	31.2	7.0	20.7
United States				
1971	9.8	26.4	5.5	12.0
1972	10.0	27.3	6.8	11.6
1973	10.8	29.7	5.9	11.4
1974	8.1	28.9	6.9	11.3
1975	6.5	30.0	6.5	12.7
1976	7.2	30.0	6.7	12.6
1977	6.9	27.0	6.4	9.9
Japan				
1971	7.0	30.2	41.5	43.4
1972	6.7	31.0	38.9	45.5
1973	6.0	29.8	31.7	46.9
1974	5.1	28.7	32.8	47.9
1975	5.0	27.5	33.2	48.6
1976	4.4	28.7	32.2	49.0
1977	4.1	30.6	31.5	53.1

Source: UN Commodity Trade tapes. Figures are rounded.

U.S. share of the ASEAN market rose. But this does not necessarily imply that U.S. competitiveness in ASEAN countries improved.

By assuming that the United States and Japan would maintain the same share of each type of product in 1977 that they had in 1971, one can compute a hypothetical export total for each country, which can then be compared with actual exports to provide a rough estimate of competitiveness. This calculation indicates that despite the strong U.S. export performance, actual U.S. exports fell short of those expected by 7.1 percent, whereas actual Japanese exports were 1 percent greater than those expected. More specifically, actual U.S. exports of natural resource and human capital products did worse than expected, while technology and unskilled labor products did slightly better. And actual Japanese exports of natural resource and labor products did worse than expected, while technology and human capital products did better. Thus each country gained competitiveness in technology products and in one other category, and lost competitiveness in natural resource products and in one other category. But on balance Japan gained and the United States lost competitiveness.

This judgment, however, is deceptive, since neither country could supply petroleum, which dominated changes in ASEAN natural resource imports. A recalculation that excluded natural resources showed that in the period 1971–77 the United States exported 9.6 percent more, and Japan 6.8 percent more, than expected, the share of nonresource goods being held constant. The better U.S. result came from success in exporting high-technology products: over the period the U.S. share of the ASEAN market rose from 26.4 to 27.0 percent, whereas the Japanese share rose less, from 30.2 to 30.6 percent. Nevertheless, examination of the markets for technology products in individual countries showed that the United States lost part of its share of both Indonesia's and the Philippines' technology imports. Between 1971 and 1977 the U.S. share of technology imports dropped from 19.5 to 17.6 percent in Indonesia and from 31.1 to 30.2 percent in the Philippines. The Japanese share of Indonesia's technology imports also declined, but by a lesser amount, from 31.1 to 29.8 percent, but its share in the Philippines increased from 32.5 to 32.8 percent. The magnitude of these shifts may seem small, but in rapidly growing markets they are significant.

To summarize the findings to this point, the United States on balance had good success in exporting to ASEAN countries during the 1970s. Thus the Japanese challenge was met in markets where Japan was the leading trading partner. The overall success can be attributed to winning a larger share of ASEAN imports of high-technology products. Given these results, U.S. exports to both Indonesia and the Philippines were disappointing. The disappointment came from less-than-expected exports of high-technology products to these two countries after 1973–74. No deviation or surprise was found in Japanese exports of high-technology products to the same countries.

High-Technology Products

These findings suggest that the trade of high-technology products requires greater scrutiny. For some high-technology products a variety of factors may be the basis for competitive struggles among suppliers, including performance characteristics, quality, and durability of product, training and education of local operatives and managers, and other technology transfers, along with more traditional elements like price, credit terms, and delivery times. The selling of some types of technology products depends on a firm's competitiveness in nontraditional elements and requires extensive negotiations before the sale as well as much local servicing after the product has been delivered to the customer. Other technology products, however, are sold on a traditional price-advantage basis. These "price-sensitive" products are usually homogeneous within a product class, can be specified rather clearly for contract purposes, and often entail a flow of product rather than a single shipment (or batch order). They involve high technology either because they use new processes in their production, such as in chemicals, or because they are new products, such as classes of semiconductors or transistors. Eleven of the thirty high-technology products in U.S. trade are price sensitive and nineteen are not.[12]

At the start of the 1970s, approximately 30 percent of U.S. exports of high-technology products to ASEAN (as reported by the United States) were price sensitive and 70 percent were not. By the end of the decade, over 45 percent of these exports were made up of price-sensitive items and only 55 percent were not. Thus within the technology group, price-sensitive exports grew faster than the others. One explanation for this shift might be a relative increase in the demand of ASEAN countries for price-sensitive items. An examination of ASEAN imports from the United States and Japan (as reported by ASEAN countries) shows that the imports of price-sensitive items from the United States rose from 20 percent of all technology imports from this country in 1971–72 to 33 percent in 1976–77 (table 4-4).[13] But since ASEAN imports of price-sensitive items from Japan as a share of total Japanese technology items hardly changed, moving from 35 percent in 1971–72 to 36 percent in 1976–77, this explanation is not valid. If there had been a general shift in ASEAN demand, it would have affected trade with Japan, the largest supplier to the market. Imports of price-sensitive technology items from Japan did increase relative to imports of other technology products in Malaysia, Singapore, and Thailand, but decreased in Indonesia and the Philippines. Imports of price-sensitive tech-

12. See the appendix for the complete list.
13. This is not identical to the finding from U.S. reported data, but the trend and amount of change is consistent.

Table 4-4. *Percentage of Price-Sensitive Products among Total Technology-Intensive Exports to ASEAN from the United States and Japan, 1971-72, 1976-77*

Country	1971-72	1976-77
ASEAN		
United States	20.2	33.0
Japan	35.0	36.0
Indonesia		
United States	19.8	23.2
Japan	39.8	37.0
Malaysia		
United States	18.5	22.6
Japan	27.4	31.0
Philippines		
United States	30.9	33.8
Japan	43.8	39.6
Singapore		
United States	11.4	38.6
Japan	27.0	33.4
Thailand		
United States	44.3	45.1
Japan	35.2	43.6
Malaysia and Singapore[a]		
United States	12.7	34.0
Japan	27.2	32.4

Source: UN Commodity Trade tapes.

a. A cross check of data of the same trade flows as reported by the United States indicates some gross inconsistencies with those reported by ASEAN. Since the differences appear to be in the destination of U.S. exports as between Malaysia and Singapore, the data for the two countries have been combined.

nology items from the United States showed a relative increase in all the ASEAN countries, including Indonesia and the Philippines.

A closer examination of each of the thirty technology-intensive products reveals some interesting peculiarities. U.S. exports of these products to all destinations increased over fourfold between 1970 and 1979. To ASEAN countries, the increase was over ninefold. Furthermore, the percentage increase in exports for each individual product was greater to ASEAN countries than to the world except for three items—chemical elements, fertilizer, and tractors—that are all price sensitive. Therefore, the relatively disappointing increase in U.S. exports of non-price-sensitive high-technology products to Indonesia and the Philippines was not due to some overall U.S. competitive disadvantage in ASEAN countries that happened to be reflected in trade with these two countries.[14]

A product-by-product review of the data indicates that eight products in Indonesia and eight products in the Philippines were export disappointments. That is, for each of these products the United States lost market shares during the 1970s in either Indonesia or the Philippines while gaining market shares in the other ASEAN countries. Six of the eight products for both Indonesia and the Philippines were not price sensitive.[15] Thus the evidence suggests that U.S. exporters had particular difficulty in selling certain non-price-sensitive high-technology products to these two countries.

Two possible explanations of these findings come to mind. Either U.S. exporters became more price competitive relative to the other aspects of competitiveness, or U.S. exporters suffered a deterioration in their ability to compete in the nonprice aspects of high-technology products. The first possibility provides a plausible hypothesis. The dollar was devalued early in the 1970s and was depreciated further after generalized floating of currencies was adopted. U.S. products must then have become more price competitive, even though U.S. domestic inflation was above the average of other industrial countries, and devaluation by itself would not change any of the other aspects of competitiveness. Therefore, U.S. exports of price-sensitive items might have done better than other exports. However, the consequence of the dollar's devaluation relative to the yen and the German mark was effective in all the ASEAN countries, not in just three of them. As noted previously, the United States export disappointment was in technology exports only to Indonesia and the Philippines. This hypothesis does not shed any light on that finding, although it does help explain some of the generally good performance.

14. The reported destination of exports in U.S. data may contain systematic errors. Exports shipped to Singapore, for example, may be sent to a regional distributor there and then transshipped to Indonesia. To overcome this problem, import data from each of the ASEAN countries were used in preference to U.S. export data.

15. Four of the products were the same for both countries. The export disappointments to Indonesia were 'other' chemicals, transistors, jet engines, office machines, metal working machinery, electric power machinery, electrical medical equipment, and optical products. The export disappointments in the Philippines were plastics, agricultural machinery, office machines, metal working machinery, electric power machinery, telecommunications equipment, electric medical equipment, and aircraft.

The second possibility, that United States exporters suffered a deterioration in the nonprice elements of competition, is the explanation frequently mentioned by American business people operating in the region.[16] Many have drawn attention to the disincentives introduced into U.S. law and administrative practice by the U.S. government, particularly in the second half of the 1970s. The Foreign Corrupt Practices Act, the taxation of American citizens residing abroad, and the introduction of human rights criteria into Export-Import Bank loans and other government dealings since 1975 are often cited along with longer-standing concerns over the extraterritorial aspects of U.S. antitrust laws. It is suggested that these laws and administrative practices constitute a powerful disincentive to U.S. exports, since they prevent American firms from conducting their foreign business with American employees in conformity with local practice. Insofar as these factors do work as export disincentives, they are likely to weigh particularly heavily on non-price-sensitive technology products in which each contract requires much negotiation and involves large sums of money.

These disincentives are likely to be greatest in countries where central government administration is weak and no tradition of independent local government exists. They are also likely to be a function of economic development itself, since weak administration is more often found in countries at an early stage of development. Among ASEAN countries, Singapore does not constitute a problem market, because it is a well-administered city-state that has reached a high level of development. Malaysia, which has built on the traditional civil service inherited from Great Britain and molded that service to its needs, is also not a problem area. Business practice in Thailand, however, does create problems for American firms operating under the new U.S. laws, though the situation is moderated somewhat because Thailand is geographically rather small, is a contiguous landmass, and has a long history as a nation state.

It is in Indonesia and the Philippines that the problems are particularly severe. Both countries are made up of many islands with separate cultures and distinct languages, where central administration is difficult under the best of circumstances. These factors, combined with the recent history of indigenous conflicts and authoritarian politics in both countries, have created a mosaic of business practice in which the idealized Western version of arm's-length dealing is more the exception than the rule. Many stories are told of the need to make local side payments or payoffs to local officials.

16. A mail survey was conducted of all the members of the ASEAN-U.S. Business Council. Almost all of them responded themselves or directed someone in their company to respond.

There is anecdotal evidence that some American business firms found the situation so difficult that they decided to abandon their business in either or both countries after the passage of the new U.S. laws, although other businesses seem to be able to operate without violating those laws. Thus U.S. export disincentives do provide a plausible explanation for the relatively disappointing U.S. export performance of high-technology products to Indonesia and the Philippines.

Conclusion

More is at stake here than the success or lack of success of U.S. exports of some particular products to some particular markets. The big question is how the United States is going to adjust to the tremendous changes that are occurring in the world economy and whether the U.S. economy is likely to benefit from them or be harmed by them. When world energy prices change or when developing countries create a capacity to produce manufactured products that are competitive in world markets, all countries must and will make adjustments. The balance of payments will ultimately be adjusted if by no other means than by changes in exchange rates. But the economic consequences will differ depending on the nature of the changes and the kind of adjustment undertaken.

The adjustments in U.S. export structure during the 1970s is reflected in table 4-1. Since the United States was an importer of energy (net), the adjustment to the deterioration in the U.S. terms of trade had to be a rise in the value of U.S. exports relative to imports. This was inevitable and has occurred. But which American exports expanded relative to others, and what are the implications for U.S. welfare? As previously mentioned, the immediate and partially sustained adjustment in U.S. exports to all destinations during the 1970s was a rise in exports of natural resource–intensive products. This is an appropriate response. It builds on a growing American comparative advantage in producing temperate agricultural products; it reflects the passing along of higher energy costs into the prices of energy-intensive products; and it demonstrates the newly enhanced competitiveness of American energy exports like coal.

The adjustment, however, also took the form of slightly larger U.S. exports of labor-intensive products. For several years, in contrast to other industrial countries, the United States suffered a decline in real wages because nominal wages rose less than the inflation rate. So when the dollar was devalued, which adjusted the average difference in overall inflations, U.S. exports of labor-intensive products such as textiles became more competitive in the markets of other industrial countries. In the case of textiles, industrial countries have import barriers against imports from developing countries, but not against those from other industrial countries. Meanwhile U.S. exports of technology-intensive products remained about the same, but apparently U.S. exports of human capital–intensive products declined. Granting the difficulty of giving empirical content to the theoretical concept of human capital–intensive products, if these exports did decline in favor of labor-intensive products, then the adjustment reflects a diminution of U.S. economic welfare. If, for example, the United States substitutes production of textiles and shoes for that of automobiles, the productivity of the country declines, as does the average real income of its citizens.

As already noted, the adjustment of U.S. exports to the ASEAN countries was different and much healthier for the U.S. economy. In these countries high-technology products accounted for the expansion of U.S. exports. Substitution of production of high-technology goods for other types of goods is desirable for the U.S. economy, since it is likely to improve productivity and welfare. And rapidly growing countries, especially newly developing ones, are likely to be the best markets for high-technology products. Consequently, the U.S. economy may seriously suffer if the problems that American firms have had in exporting high-technology products to Indonesia and the Philippines occur in other developing countries.

Chapter Five

U.S. Services and Direct Investment

The dynamic ASEAN countries have attracted the attention of many American companies. As described in chapter 4, this has led to the outstanding growth of U.S. exports of merchandise to these countries. It has also resulted in the growth of service exports to them and, to a lesser extent, of direct investment in them. The exports of services, merchandise, and direct investment are functionally related and in some cases cannot be separated. Thus it is not surprising that all three are increasing. Indeed, half the members of the ASEAN-U.S. Business Council are associated with companies in the service business. This chapter reviews U.S. exports of services to ASEAN countries and direct investment in them and compares these flows, when possible, with similar flows from Japan.

Services

For several decades the United States has been moving toward a service-oriented economy. It was estimated that in 1981 service industries made up two-thirds of U.S. gross national product and employed 70 percent of all workers.[1] One would expect this trend to be reflected in U.S. economic relations with other countries, including ASEAN countries. Many services cannot enter international commerce, however, and others, like education, are not reported as exports of service.[2] Nonetheless, the apparent shift in U.S. production is likely to be reflected in improved international comparative advantage in services. Already it seems to be reflected in trends in the

1. Office of the United States Trade Representative, "Brock Urges Service Industries to Export," press release, April 20, 1981.
2. For example, McGraw-Hill, Inc., leases rights to correspondence courses to the Philippine Technikum, which also markets other lower-level technical programs in English of the American company, but the transactions are not recorded separately, nor are expenditures of ASEAN students in American universities. Marci Kenney, "Current Developments and Trends in International Educational Services" (U.S. Department of Commerce, International Trade Administration, June 1981).

U.S. balance of payments, as noted below. It is consistent with the evidence that U.S. exports of merchandise as a share of goods-and-service exports declined from 71.5 percent in 1960 to 66.7 percent in 1970 and to 64.2 percent in 1980, whereas U.S. imports of merchandise as a share of goods-and-service imports rose from 63.1 percent in 1960 to 67.2 percent in 1970 and to 78.8 percent in 1980.

The nonmerchandise part of goods and services includes both factor income, like interest and dividends from foreign investment, and service exports, with the former about twice as large as the latter. However, both have grown absolutely and in relation to merchandise exports. To be sure, the mechanism whereby Americans provide services to other countries often involves a direct investment, and therefore the service may be provided by a foreign affiliate. It has been estimated that 86 percent of U.S. service sales abroad result from foreign affiliates.[3] Hence service exports and that part of factor income coming from certain direct investments are difficult to distinguish.

The U.S. Department of Commerce has identified the U.S. services that are significant in world commerce: accounting, advertising, banking, communications, computer, construction and engineering, consulting and management, education, employment, franchising, health, insurance, legal, motion pictures, shipping and air transport, and tourism (including hotel and motel).[4] The striking feature of these services is their heterogeneity, which makes it difficult to design an information-gathering system for them. Only in recent years has any effort been made to do so. Therefore, little is known with certainty about the international trade of services, especially in specific areas like ASEAN. But several trends are believed to exist. First, international business apparently makes up a growing share of the total activities of many U.S. service industries.[5] Second, international competition for this business is increasing, with Japan being one of the main competitors of the United States. Third, many of the service industries face growing difficulties in operating abroad because of either the policies or the inactiveness of the U.S. government, and because of restrictions in host countries.

3. U.S. Department of Commerce, Office of the Assistant Secretary for Policy, *U.S. Service Industries in World Markets: Current Problems and Future Policy Developments* (Government Printing Office, 1976), p. 17.
4. U.S. Department of Commerce, International Trade Administration, *Current Developments in U.S. International Service Industries* (GPO, 1980).
5. Industry surveys that indicate this trend exist for some services like accounting. Ibid., pp. 12–14.

The only sources of U.S. information that identify ASEAN countries separately are the two censuses of U.S. direct investment abroad taken for the years 1966 and 1977.[6] Through them some estimate of the growth of U.S. service business in ASEAN countries is possible. Of course, these data cover only that business conducted by foreign affiliates.[7]

In 1966 the U.S. direct investment position in affiliates in the service business in ASEAN countries was valued at $60 million. Almost 80 percent of the investment was in the Philippines. From that investment the U.S. parent companies earned profits of about $7 million and also received payments of about $9 million for royalties and fees.[8] In 1977 the American direct investment position had risen to $364 million in service industries, which implies a growth rate of almost 18 percent a year over the eleven-year span between censuses.[9] By 1977 the distribution of U.S. investment among the ASEAN countries was widespread, and the Philippine concentration had declined to less than 50 percent. This rate of growth compares favorably with what happened in merchandise trade.

U.S. parent companies earned $92 million on this investment in 1977 and received about $24 million in fees and royalties.[10] These figures are somewhat misleading, since much of the earnings arose out of the banking business. There are two problems. One, external borrowing by affiliate banks through which loans are made and interest earned is made possible in part because the capital of the parent bank either explicitly or implicitly stands behind the affiliate. And two, when a new branch is opened, it is standard practice to shift loans already made to that country from the books of the parent to the affiliate so that the affiliate gets a good start. Because Singapore began to emerge as an international banking center during this period and attracted many U.S. banks, and Manila also encouraged the development of offshore banking, the start-up phenomenon could be significant.

Another interesting fragment of information on American service industries in ASEAN relates to the advertising industry. Of the top ten U.S. advertising agencies, two operate in Indonesia, four in the Philippines, five

6. U.S. Department of Commerce, Bureau of Economic Analysis, *U.S. Direct Investment Abroad, 1977* (GPO 1981); and U.S. Department of Commerce, Bureau of Economic Analysis, *U.S. Direct Investment Abroad, 1966, Final Data* (GPO, n.d.).

7. Direet export of services may follow the same trend as affiliates except for tourist services, for which U.S. data do not distinguish ASEAN countries.

8. Bureau of Economic Analysis, *U.S. Direct Investment Abroad, 1966*, pp. 31, 69, 76.

9. Bureau of Economic Analysis, *U.S. Direct Investment Abroad, 1977*, p. 46.

10. Ibid., pp. 83, 97.

each in Singapore and Thailand, and six in Malaysia. This implies significant U.S. interest in ASEAN. However, the Japanese competition is strengthening. The advertising agency with the world's largest gross worldwide income in 1977 was Japanese (Dentsu), and nine other Japanese agencies are among the fifty world leaders.[11] Thus Japan is probably a strong competitor in ASEAN for the advertising business.

The difficulties facing American providers of services in ASEAN countries are as varied as the services themselves. Some exist for all affiliates, but others are industry specific. For instance, control and regulation is common in the banking business as well as discrimination in favor of domestic banks. Even so, the environment in ASEAN countries is relatively favorable for international banking, and American banks have had few special difficulties that seriously inhibit their operation.

Likewise in insurance and reinsurance, host countries put limits on the ability of foreign companies to compete. The Philippines and Malaysia, which favor state-owned reinsurance companies, require compulsory reinsurance concessions to the state reinsurer, place restrictions on remittances and on contract enforceability and servicing, and give directives on the localization of funds; the Philippines also puts limits on placing insurance abroad.[12] There is nothing unusual in any of these regulations. The reinsurance business has been a growth area in international commerce, an area in which the Japanese are increasingly competitive. Potential competition and discrimination could come from an effort to create an ASEAN insurer and reinsurer to operate in all member countries. Already the Asian Reinsurance Corporation has been set up in Bangkok with the backing of the United Nations Conference on Trade and Development (UNCTAD).[13] Like many other developing nations, the ASEAN countries have been placing increasing limitations on the ability of foreign firms to write marine insurance, even though this type of insurance has not been profitable in recent years.

Some of the important policy issues regarding services relate to the overseas operations of American construction and engineering companies. These companies attract particular attention because they generate large exports of goods as well as services. Of course, the major expansion of this

11. International Trade Administration, *Current Developments in U.S. International Service Industries*, p. 26.

12. Robert L. Carter and Gerard M. Dickinson, *Barriers to Trade in Insurance*, Thames Essay 19 (London: Trade Policy Research Centre, 1979).

13. International Trade Administration, *Current Developments in U.S. International Service Industries*, p. 82.

Table 5-1. U.S. Direct Investment: Total Assets of Foreign Affiliates in 1977 and 1966

Millions of U.S. dollars

Year and country	All industries	Mining	Petroleum	Manufacturing								Trade	Banking	Finance	Other
				Total	Food	Chemicals	Primary and fabricated metals	Machinery and electricity	Electrical machinery	Trans-portation	Other				
1977															
All countries	145,990	5,998	28,030	62,019	5,571	11,864	4,626	11,223	5,494	9,321	13,921	16,836	4,370	21,248	7,489
Indonesia	984	a	736	97	2	30	a	*	13	*	a	9	8	5	a
Malaysia	464	4	a	86	3	15	2	4	46	*	15	a	8	2	14
Philippines	837	*	273	317	100	88	14	1	34	a	a	76	93	26	52
Singapore	516	0	232	106	5	3	28	15	45	1	9	75	49	18	37
Thailand	237	6	a	51	9	9	4	0	11	*	18	a	27	6	8
ASEAN	3,038	10	1,241	657	119	145	48	20	149	1	42	160	185	57	111
1966															
All countries	51,792	3,983	13,893	20,740	1,771	3,840	1,448	5,033	...	3,919	4,728	4,331	4,540		2,046
Indonesia	106	4	97	0	0	0	0	0	...	0	0	*	2		7
Malaysia	57	4	26	6	1	−1	0	3	...	0	3	6	a		a
Philippines	486	a	a	166	44	46	4	17	...	0	55	69	9		34
Singapore	30	0	a	4	*	*	*	3	...	0	*	a	*		*
Thailand	51	0	a	18	2	2	a	1	...	0	a	a	4		5
ASEAN	730	4	123	194	47	47	4	24	...	0	58	75	15		46

Sources: U.S. Department of Commerce, Bureau of Economic Analysis, *U.S. Direct Investment Abroad, 1977* (Government Printing Office, 1981), p. 46; and U.S. Department of Commerce, Bureau of Economic Analysis, *U.S. Direct Investment Abroad, 1966, Final Data* (GPO, n.d.), p. 31.

*Less than $500,000.

a. Suppressed by Bureau of Economic Analysis for purposes of confidentiality.

business in recent years has occurred in OPEC countries, and especially in Saudi Arabia. Nevertheless, all the rapidly growing developing countries have been good markets. The less-developed countries—particularly South Korea—are also providing new stiff competition. Within ASEAN, Philippine construction companies have been active competitors of American ones.

Many American companies complain that they are at a disadvantage in competing for international contracts because the U.S. government does not match the support given foreign companies by their governments. Japan, for example, is noted for providing project money to aid its companies in obtaining contracts. Furthermore, American companies have been hindered by such U.S. government restrictions as tax provisions, export licensing provisions, antiboycott restrictions, the Foreign Corrupt Practices Act, rules relating to procurement under U.S. aid programs, and requirements concerning human rights and environmental impact.[14] Most of these apply to doing business in ASEAN countries. Because the construction industry is so important and can affect the whole U.S. economy, its complaints should not be ignored.

Direct Investment

U.S. direct investment in the Philippines has existed for many years because of colonial ties. U.S. investment was also centrally involved in developing the petroleum industry in Indonesia during the 1950s. But U.S. interest in investment in other ASEAN countries, and in manufacturing investment in general, is of quite recent origin. In 1966 the U.S. direct investment position in all ASEAN countries amounted to only $730 million (table 5-1). Two-thirds of the total was invested in the Philippines and 13 percent in Indonesian oil, leaving only 20 percent for everything else. U.S. firms had invested just $30 million in Singapore and only about $50 million each in Malaysia and Thailand. Together ASEAN countries made up only 1.4 percent of total U.S. foreign investment in 1966.

By the time the next census was taken in 1977, the situation had begun to change, but by no means has there been a great flow of U.S. investment into these countries. The U.S. direct investment position in ASEAN countries in 1977 amounted to $3 billion, which indicates a growth rate of 13.7 percent a year since 1966. This is somewhat greater than the 9.9 percent

14. Ibid., p. 59.

annual growth rate for worldwide U.S. investment, but less than might have been expected given the dynamic growth of the ASEAN economies. Because of slow growth in U.S. investment in the Philippines, that country's share declined to 28 percent of the ASEAN total. By contrast, U.S. investment in Singapore boomed, growing annually at a 30 percent rate. It is notable that Singapore accepted foreign investment as the critical element in its development strategy. It is the only country in ASEAN that does not insist on local participation in ownership and has few other restrictions as long as the investment fits into the government's development strategy.[15] U.S. firms have responded by investing in such industries as petroleum refining, machinery manufacturing, and electrical parts assembly.

Japanese firms have been rapidly increasing their investment in ASEAN countries; it has been estimated that in 1976 more than three-quarters of all new foreign investment was Japanese.[16] In 1966 Japanese firms had invested only $166 million in ASEAN countries, less than one-quarter the value of U.S. investment. But by the end of 1976, Japanese investment had reached $4 billion, one-third larger than U.S. investment, and had increased by $1 billion in 1976 alone.[17] It has been further estimated that Japanese investment had exceeded $7 billion by the end of 1980, whereas U.S. investment had reached only about $5 billion.[18] Much of Japanese investment is concentrated in Indonesia and is involved in the production and processing of natural resources, but Japan also has a significant investment position in the other ASEAN countries. According to a 1976 survey, Japanese investment was more than twice as large as that of the United States in Thailand and Indonesia and 50 percent larger in Malaysia, but only three-quarters as large in the Philippines and less than half as large in Singapore.[19] However, the level of Japanese investment in Sin-

15. Rupert Pennant-Rea, "Who Pays the Piper: A Survey of Foreign Investment in Asia," *Economist*, June 23–29, 1979.

16. Ibid.

17. Figures come from the Japanese Ministry of Finance, *Fiscal and Monetary Statistics Monthly*, no. 305 (September 1977), cited by Sueo Sekiguchi and Lawrence B. Krause, "Direct Foreign Investment in ASEAN by Japan and the United States," in Ross Garnaut, ed., *ASEAN in a Changing Pacific and World Economy* (Miami: Australian National University Press, 1980), p. 428. Figures represent approved, rather than actual, investment expenditures.

18. For Japanese figures, *Look Japan*, August 10, 1981, p. 9; for U.S. figures, statement of Charles W. Robinson, in *U.S. Policy in Southeast Asia*, Hearings before the Subcommittee on East Asian and Pacific Affairs of the Senate Committee on Foreign Relations, 97 Cong. 1 sess. (GPO, 1981), pp. 44–55.

19. Japan External Trade Organization, *White Paper on Overseas Markets, 1977*, vol. 2 (Tokyo: JETRO, 1977).

gapore more than doubled in the three-year period 1978–80 and is now approaching the level of U.S. investment.

Why has Japanese direct investment increased faster than that of U.S. firms in ASEAN countries? Part of the answer may simply be that the Japanese economy has performed better than the U.S. economy in recent years. Japanese firms have earned greater profits than their American counterparts and have had access to greater amounts of savings, so they have been more able and willing to invest both at home and abroad.

Part of the answer, however, lies in the differences between U.S. and Japanese direct investment.[20] American firms undertake natural resource investment as part of their worldwide strategy to serve world markets. The American firms that invest in manufacturing abroad are usually quite large and belong to oligopolistic industries, and the investment frequently involves sophisticated technology that provides the necessary competitive edge to succeed in an alien environment. American firms sell their output primarily in local or regional markets.

Japanese firms, on the other hand, invest abroad to obtain secure sources of natural resources for export back to resource-deficient Japan, although in Indonesia, Thailand, and the Philippines investment to allow the local market to overcome the barriers of an import-replacement development strategy was important as well.[21] Japanese firms also invest in manufacturing abroad to reduce their wage costs; they thus tend to be involved in older, labor-intensive industries rather than large-scale, capital-intensive ones. Japanese firms operating abroad obtain their competitive edge through their marketing skills and, in particular, through their ability to export to Japan, which few foreign firms can do. That is why Japanese trading companies usually join Japanese manufacturing firms in foreign ventures. ASEAN, along with Korea and Taiwan, is a natural site for such investment. ASEAN countries are located close to Japan, which minimizes transportation and communication costs. They have many underdeveloped natural resources and reasonably low wages. It is no wonder that Japanese firms have invested so heavily there.

Still, ASEAN countries should be more attractive to U.S. investors than they appear to have been. From the data available, it would appear that the American firms that have invested in ASEAN countries have done quite

20. Sekiguchi and Krause, "Direct Foreign Investment in ASEAN by Japan and the United States," pp. 421–52.

21. Kunio Yoshihara, *Japanese Investment in Southeast Asia*, Monograph of the Center for Southeast Asian Studies, Kyoto University (University Press of Hawaii, 1978), chap. 3.

well.[22] Reported earnings on U.S. direct investment in ASEAN countries rose from $63 million in 1966 to $1.2 billion in 1977, about a 30 percent annual rate of growth. This compares favorably with the 14.7 percent growth rate of earnings of total U.S. direct investment. The petroleum industry was the main source of earnings growth in ASEAN countries, no doubt aided by the rise of oil prices in 1973–74. But profits in manufacturing also increased rapidly at a 24 percent annual rate in ASEAN countries as against the 15.1 percent annual rate of growth of profits of total U.S. direct investment in manufacturing. U.S. earnings in manufacturing in Singapore have advanced particularly well and, though the value of the investment is lower, now exceed those in the Philippines. The relative stagnation of American investment in the Philippines may be due to the less favorable income experience, even though investment in the Philippines compares well with the average return of American manufacturing investment in all countries. Or perhaps the same factors are at work that inhibited American exports of high-technology products to the Philippines and Indonesia, as discussed in chapter 4.

It is generally believed that American firms have not taken full advantage of the investment opportunities available to them in ASEAN countries and that, relatively, they are losing out to their Japanese competitors. Mari Pangestu calculates that the importance of U.S. investment is declining in all ASEAN countries except Malaysia.[23] According to Pangestu, while Japan shows positive bias in investing in ASEAN countries (that is, greater investment than could be attributed to factor complementarities between Japan and ASEAN countries), the United States shows low and declining levels of bias. If this perception is correct, should the United States be concerned from the society's point of view? Clearly some elements of U.S. society do not favor foreign investment, believing that such investment weakens the U.S. balance of payments and reduces employment in the United States. Extensive research efforts to date, however, have failed to substantiate such negative effects on the U.S. economy.[24] Rather, the

22. Earnings data should be interpreted with care. The asset base is calculated at inflation-distorted historical values. Furthermore, some earnings flows may be disguised in other payments to circumvent repatriation restrictions. Earnings are reported in the census reports. Ibid.

23. Mari Pangestu, *Japanese and Other Foreign Investment in the ASEAN Countries*, Australia-Japan Research Centre Research Paper 73 (Australian National University Press, n.d.), p. 2.

24. C. Fred Bergsten, Thomas Horst, and Theodore H. Moran, *American Multinationals and American Interests* (Brookings Institution, 1978).

American firms that compete best for international markets are those that invest abroad as well as export from the United States. Foreign investment seems to be an integral part of staying abreast of world competitive developments, and firms that do not make foreign investments usually take little interest in selling abroad. If the United States is to meet the Japanese challenge in the ASEAN countries, then, American firms will have to invest in them as well as export to them.

It is also clear that ASEAN governments welcome U.S. investment.[25] They desire it not only to promote growth and employment and to improve technology but also to counterbalance Japanese investment and lessen their dependence on Japan. As evidence of this, ASEAN governments made representation to the U.S. government to ensure favorable tax treatment for U.S. firms when investing in ASEAN countries. Of course, as already noted, ASEAN governments do restrict investments by foreigners in various ways, but these restrictions are not aimed solely or principally at U.S. firms. In fact, the reverse may be true. The disagreements of ASEAN countries with multinational firms have been muted as the firms have become more aware of local needs. Multinational firms recognize the ASEAN countries' desire for economic development, while ASEAN governments recognize the firms' need for profit.[26] This mutual understanding has become the basis for a constructive relationship. In view of this favorable climate, American firms should be prepared to make greater investments in the future.

25. Lloyd R. Vasey, ed., *ASEAN and a Positive Strategy for Foreign Investment* (University Press of Hawaii for the Pacific Forum, 1978).

26. Pennant-Rea, "Who Pays the Piper."

Chapter Six

Principles for U.S. Policy

ASEAN is more important to the United States than is generally realized. ASEAN countries are the prototype of advanced developing countries, whose progress and problems will dominate the world economic scene during the last two decades of the twentieth century. If the United States is able to formulate and implement a successful policy for handling economic relations with them, then a giant stride will have been taken in sustaining and enhancing the U.S. role in the world economy.

U.S. policy must recognize two fundamental facts. For one thing, no matter how successful President Reagan's economic policy turns out to be, the economic hegemony of the United States over the world economy has ended and cannot be reestablished. This has several implications. First, other countries are less affected by what goes on in the U.S. economy than they once were. American economic expansions, for instance, are no longer sufficient to ignite the world economy, nor do American recessions necessarily cause acute distress. Thus the United States can now be out of step with other countries, which gives it greater leeway in formulating policy. Second, the United States is no longer the only source of sophisticated machinery, nor necessarily the developer of the most advanced industrial technology. Therefore, direct investment by American firms is not the only channel through which countries can receive technology transfers. Third, American banks no longer dominate the list of the world's largest financial institutions, nor are they the predominant source of international loans. Hence American firms must compete more aggressively with foreign enterprises and American policy must permit and encourage them to do so.

The other significant fact is that the U.S. economy itself is greatly dependent on world economic forces. Other countries have long been aware of such dependency vis-à-vis their own economies, but dependency is relatively new to the United States. It is the natural consequence of world interdependence, which is the basis of a high standard of living.

The combination of the decline in U.S. influence on the world economy and the greater dependence of the U.S. economy on others requires a shift in U.S. economic strategy and policies. In the past the United States has been active in initiating global international economic policies, but passive in responding to the policy actions of others. This position must now be reversed: the United States must exercise caution in initiating policy but be very active in adjusting its policy to events abroad and to the policy actions of others.

The global economy is still of great concern to the United States, but responsibility for formulating global policies must be shared collectively, not dominated by the United States. Indeed, other countries may have more compelling reasons to take responsibility for some global structures than the United States has. For example, Japan is now the natural leader in determining global policy for international trade. If Japan responds to trade problems by restricting trade, world trade will inevitably become more restricted. But if Japan is prepared to liberalize trade, further growth of world trade can be encouraged. Japan has the domestic economic strength to initiate policy; it has great economic interest in sustaining open world markets; and because of its relatively closed economy for imports of manufactured products, it has sufficient bargaining chips to induce other nations to negotiate for further liberalization. The United States is less well positioned in each of these respects. But if the United States always insists on proposing new global policies itself rather than having patience and waiting for Japan to do so, Japan will not have the incentive to take initiatives.

U.S. policymakers must feel free to formulate appropriate policies for regions or subregions like the Caribbean or ASEAN without greater concern for their effect on global structures than that felt by other countries. With respect to ASEAN, the United States will have to pay close attention to Japan and design policies that will enable it to stay in the competitive race with Japan. That may require some region-specific policies, which, however, need not be overtly discriminatory to other countries. Fears about giving less attention to the global economy should not stand in the way of proper regional policy. Indeed, if global economic relations should begin to sour, regional arrangements would be the second-best alternative.

This chapter reviews the findings of this study and discusses economic relations between ASEAN and the United States from an ASEAN perspective. The record of the U.S. response to ASEAN is also described and the goals of U.S. policy enumerated. In the final chapter specific policy problems are discussed and recommendations made.

Findings of the Study

The ASEAN countries are among the fastest growing countries of the world. For the last fifteen years, the economic growth rates of Indonesia, Malaysia, the Philippines, Singapore, and Thailand have been as high on average as those of the OPEC countries and the newly industrializing countries of Asia and Latin America, and higher than that of Japan, the most successful industrial country. Moreover, the ASEAN countries have a combined population larger than that of the United States, indicating their potential as producers and consumers. The level of income already achieved in these countries is rather low, with the notable exception of Singapore. The other four countries are still classified by the World Bank as middle-income countries (Indonesia is actually at the upper edge of low-income countries). Most observers believe that rapid growth will continue for some time, and in my view the growth rates of ASEAN countries will exceed those of other countries except for several that are also in the Pacific basin, like Hong Kong and South Korea.

The ASEAN countries are of great political and strategic importance in themselves because they straddle crucial sea-lanes and are neighbors of troubled Indochina. The United States stations military forces in the Philippines under treaty, has an explicit security commitment to Thailand under the Manila Pact, and implicitly defends the others from hostile external threats. Thus U.S. economic policy for ASEAN has an important political and strategic dimension.[1]

As an institution, the Association of Southeast Asian Nations has existed since 1967, but it became vibrant only after the fall of Saigon in 1975. Unlike other efforts at economic integration among less-developed countries, ASEAN is likely to be sustained: it is a political necessity for the member countries and has an important role in preserving the stability of the region.

The economic program of ASEAN as an institution is still underdeveloped and probably got off on the wrong foot because of some less-than-optimal approaches to integration. Nevertheless, closer economic ties are evolving among the members, and institutional arrangements are also likely to develop, albeit slowly and pragmatically.

ASEAN is sustained in part through the interest and attention given it by other countries. Japan, Australia, Canada, New Zealand, and the Euro-

1. Larry A. Niksch, *The Association of Southeast Asian Nations (ASEAN): An Emerging Challenge in U.S. Policy towards Asia* (Congressional Research Service, 1978).

pean Community as well as the United States have created institutional ties to it. Most recently, South Korea has established closer relations. China, Vietnam, and the Soviet Union have also shown interest in ASEAN.

The economic interaction between the United States and the ASEAN countries has progressed rapidly in recent years. U.S. efforts to expand exports of merchandise to the ASEAN countries have achieved notable success. The United States has captured a large and growing share of the ASEAN market (excluding petroleum). Furthermore, the portion of U.S. exports to the ASEAN countries made up of technology-intensive products has risen dramatically. To be able to export these products is of great value to the United States, since they promote growth in the U.S. standard of living. Nevertheless, problems have arisen in U.S. exports of high-technology products to Indonesia and the Philippines, problems that appear to be related to the new U.S. policies introduced during the mid-1970s and embodied in the Foreign Corrupt Practices Act and other legislation.

While less is known about U.S. exports of services to ASEAN countries, fragmentary evidence suggests that they are also expanding. However, Japanese competition is increasing and may well impinge on the position of U.S. firms in the future.

As for direct investment in ASEAN countries, Japanese firms have already surpassed American firms and are in the process of establishing a dominant position. U.S. investment is still large, however, and second only to that of Japan. But if Japanese firms steadily increase their investment margin over U.S. firms, the continued growth of U.S. exports of goods and services will be threatened, since they are usually closely related to foreign investment.

The ASEAN countries and ASEAN as an institution have been taken seriously by American business firms. These firms were instrumental in setting up the ASEAN-U.S. Business Council in 1979 and have had several successful meetings with their ASEAN counterparts. The U.S. government also sponsored an investment mission to ASEAN (under the aegis of the Overseas Private Investment Corporation), which elicited strong business support.

Both Japanese business and the Japanese government have made significant efforts to increase and solidify Japanese economic interest in ASEAN countries. These countries have been a test case for a more aggressive style of Japanese diplomacy that is made possible by and is more in conformity with Japan's economic superpower status.

ASEAN Needs and Desires

In order to be successful, U.S. policy will have to be compatible with the desires and goals that the ASEAN countries have set for themselves. Each country still views itself as fully independent and has only marginally constrained its sovereignty for the purposes of ASEAN. In fact, each wants to enhance its bilateral relations with the United States, not submerge them in ASEAN. Nevertheless, ASEAN as an institution is important to all the members. They recognize that their external security is promoted through ASEAN unity. For example, their united position has forestalled foreign recognition of the Vietnamese-supported Heng Samrin regime in Kampuchea, one of the measures considered necessary to prevent the permanent domination of Kampuchea by Vietnam. A unified stand on the care and resettlement of Indochinese refugees has also brought greater attention to that issue and resulted in prompter world reaction to it. ASEAN unity has even affected the economic conflict with Australia over international civil aviation policy, which resulted in a satisfactory outcome for the ASEAN countries.[2] For these countries, ASEAN provides a way to institutionalize consultations on regional security matters, to overcome any residual tensions among the members themselves, and to achieve economic gains. ASEAN has the potential for making the economic position of each of the member countries better than it would otherwise have been.

The member countries have appreciated the role the United States has played in supporting ASEAN. But they know that external recognition is not enough to guarantee ASEAN's viability. Aware that ASEAN unity is fragile, they are unlikely to want to put it at risk.

Although their external economic goals differ somewhat, all the member countries identify with third world issues. Indonesia was a cofounder of the nonaligned movement, which remains an important element in its foreign policy. All the members are part of the Group of 77 (a loose-knit third world caucus within the United Nations) for UN purposes. And the Philippines hosted a general meeting of UNCTAD in May 1979. Thus they give support to the so-called south position in discussions of North-South issues. However, they are more pragmatic than many African, Latin American, and other Asian countries and are more inclined to want to move the discussions toward action than to maintain rhetorical purity. And unlike some

---

2. Amado A. Castro, "ASEAN Economic Co-operation," in Ross Garnaut, ed., *ASEAN in a Changing Pacific and World Economy* (Miami: Australian National University Press, 1980), pp. 53–66.

other developing countries, they have not sought to maneuver UN meetings into deadlock in order to promote confrontation with the West.

Among the specific issues that have arisen under the banner of a New International Economic Order, the problem of primary commodities has been most important to ASEAN countries. Their economies remain heavily dependent on the production and export of commodities. Even Singapore, as processor and transshipper of commodities, is involved. Because changes in the price and volume of commodity exports tend to be positively correlated, the value of commodity exports tends to fluctuate greatly in response to business fluctuations in industrial countries.[3] ASEAN countries have been leaders in the promotion of international commodity agreements to solve this problem, especially for commodities like rubber and tin in which they dominate world production. They have been particularly concerned that the United States is unwilling to join in the renegotiated International Tin Agreement and continues to sell tin from its surplus stocks. In bilateral talks with Japan and the United States, ASEAN countries have repeatedly raised the issue of forming a commodity regime—like the Europeans provide their associated countries in STABEX—in which automatic finance (or compensation) would be provided to them if the value of commodity exports fell significantly below trend. They have also supported the idea of the common fund under UNCTAD auspices in order to finance stabilization of world commodity prices.

A second issue that concerns ASEAN countries is access to markets for their export of manufactures. This access may become even more important to them because they envision manufactured exports as critical to their growth strategies. They have in general urged trade liberalization by industrial countries and in particular the reduction of tariff escalation by stage of production. In bilateral talks ASEAN countries have expressed strong interest in the improvement of the general system of tariff preference policies of Australia, Japan, and the United States. Furthermore, they constantly warn of the dangers for all countries of new protectionist barriers in industrial countries.

The issue of resource transfers is important to ASEAN countries, but less so than issues related to trade. They are market-oriented economies and they expect the market to provide significant amounts of foreign capital to them. Nevertheless, official development assistance is of some significance to Indonesia, Thailand, and the Philippines. They also look to the

3. For a discussion of this issue with special reference to ASEAN, see John Wong, *ASEAN Economies in Perspective* (Macmillan, 1979).

Asian Development Bank and the World Bank for loans and intellectual input into their development efforts. In bilateral talks ASEAN countries have sought government support for their integration projects and assurance of continued access to private capital markets. With respect to private direct investment, which they accept and welcome, they expect their domestic development efforts to be advanced. Thus ASEAN governments have been concerned about the distribution of gains and the spread effects of direct investment, and most countries have enacted national legislation to promote them.

In general, ASEAN countries have sought external support for their integrative efforts and at a minimum have insisted on noninterference. They believe it is legitimate to try to use their unity for bargaining with industrial countries for whatever the leverage may be worth.

Formulation of U.S. Policy

The United States has some of the same disadvantages in conducting its foreign relations with ASEAN countries as Japan (discussed in chapter 3). For some people in ASEAN, the United States defaulted on a commitment when it withdrew from Vietnam. Furthermore, as interpreted in ASEAN countries, the Nixon Doctrine implied a U.S. withdrawal from the Pacific. In the early days of the Carter administration, the proposed withdrawal of American ground troops from South Korea reinforced ASEAN fears and led to strong doubts about U.S. reliability and interest in the Pacific. After the reversal of that proposal, the United States was forgiven, but the Korean troop incident has not been forgotten in ASEAN countries.

In formulating and executing foreign policy, the United States must recognize that its form of government is difficult for foreigners to understand. Even close European allies have trouble following the meaning behind every policy swing in Washington and responding appropriately to it. The difficulty arises in part from U.S. policy mistakes. Also, foreigners are frequently unable to distinguish those American policies that stem from fundamental American interests and thus are constant from one administration (and Congress) to the next from those policies that are subject to reversal. Developing countries with short institutional memories must be forgiven if they confuse the American policies that should not be taken too seriously with those that should.

Since 1977, however, the United States has followed a consistent policy toward ASEAN. But it is incumbent on the United States to make clear that the policy is based on fundamental U.S. interests. The United States benefits from peace and prosperity in the region, and as long as the member countries view ASEAN as promoting those goals, the United States should support the institution.

U.S.-ASEAN Dialogues

Five basic principles that guide U.S. policy toward Asia were enunciated in June 1977 and were linked directly to ASEAN at the time of the first U.S.-ASEAN dialogue in September 1977.[4] They are (1) that the United States is and will remain an Asian and Pacific power; (2) that the United States will continue its important role in contributing to peace and stability in Asia and in the Pacific; (3) that the United States seeks normal and friendly relations with countries in the area on the basis of reciprocity and mutual respect; (4) that the United States will pursue mutual expansion of trade and investment across the Pacific, recognizing the growing interdependence of the economies of the United States and the region; and (5) that the United States will use its influence to improve the human condition of the peoples of Asia.

At the second U.S.-ASEAN dialogue in August 1978, the United States stated that it "strongly supports the goals and aspirations of ASEAN as part of the welfare and future of Southeast Asia" and that it "is determined to help ASEAN meet its goals."[5] This idea was carried further under the Reagan administration in an aid request to assist ASEAN itself as well as certain member countries.[6] Furthermore, association status has been granted to ASEAN to allow for cumulative rules of origin under the U.S. generalized system of tariff preferences. During 1981 several high-ranking

4. Address of Secretary of State Cyrus R. Vance before the Asia Society on June 29, 1977, published in *Department of State Bulletin*, vol. 77 (August 1977), pp. 141–45; and statement of Richard N. Cooper, under secretary for economic affairs, at the U.S.-ASEAN Economic Consultations, Manila, September 8, 1977, published in *Department of State Bulletin*, vol. 77 (October 1977), pp. 595–99.

5. Statement of Secretary Vance at the second ministerial meeting between the United States and ASEAN, August 3–4, 1978, in Washington, D.C., published in *Department of State Bulletin*, vol. 78 (September 1978), pp. 19–20.

6. Michael Armacost, "FY 1982 Assistance Requests," statement before the Subcommittee on Asian and Pacific Affairs of the House Committee on Foreign Affairs, March 23, 1981, published in *Department of State Bulletin*, vol. 81 (May 1981), pp. 26–29.

members of the Reagan administration made trips to ASEAN countries, including Secretary of State Alexander Haig, who participated in the annual ASEAN foreign ministers conference in Manila in June 1981 (the so-called five plus five meeting).[7] All these recent statements and actions indicate considerable continuity in U.S. policy.

Goals of U.S. Policy

As general goals, the United States should desire close and strong relations with the governments of the ASEAN countries that are resilient enough to withstand the inevitable strains that arise from time to time among friendly countries. These relations should not be based upon the particular persons who occupy positions of leadership at the moment, but should be founded on U.S. friendship for the peoples of the region. It must be recognized that the governments of the ASEAN countries are essentially authoritarian and centrally directed. They tend to have strong executive heads but not well-developed political institutions to balance that power or to provide a sure method for the transfer of executive power. In this respect they resemble most other third world countries. In countries that have not experienced pluralistic democracy, political cultures are more receptive to authoritarian rule. With further economic development and the creation of a large middle class this situation can be expected to change. But the political institutions that do evolve are likely to be tailored to local needs, and to reflect a country's historical experience, rather than to be patterned after Western models. If this political reality is properly recognized, U.S. foreign policy can be designed to ensure close relations without compromising U.S. commitments to individual liberty and political democracy.

With respect to the economic content of foreign policy, the United States should seek to promote its own prosperity consistent with the economic growth of its trading partners. Given the rise of economic interdependence, countries must support each others' prosperity or suffer mutual impoverishment. Therefore, international trade and investment between ASEAN countries and the United States must be promoted to enhance

7. Other visitors included Vice President George Bush, Special Trade Representative William E. Brock, Under Secretary of State James L. Buckley, and Ambassador to the United Nations Jeane J. Kirkpatrick.

economic efficiency in both areas. Furthermore, the United States should be prepared to support multilateral solutions to international development problems that will be helpful to ASEAN countries. If the United States is successful in ASEAN, it will be able to meet the Japanese challenge in other areas as well.

Chapter Seven

Specific Policy Recommendations

There is much that is positive in U.S. policy toward ASEAN. The government has recognized the political and strategic importance of ASEAN and, as noted in the previous chapter, has responded in an appropriate political and diplomatic fashion.[1] Nevertheless, more can be done by the United States to promote U.S. economic interest in ASEAN and to reflect ASEAN as an institution. And while the business community has responded to opportunities in the region, American firms exporting to and operating in ASEAN countries have been successful despite an economic policy that has sometimes hindered them. Indeed, as a ten-day study mission led by Senator Lloyd M. Bentsen (Democrat of Texas) of the Joint Economic Committee to East Asia in 1980 confirmed, many Americans and foreigners believe that U.S. policy has made it increasingly difficult for American firms to compete in the region.[2] This chapter explores some of these problems and suggests ways in which U.S. policy can be improved.

Promoting U.S. Economic Interests in ASEAN

Most of the policies that might be pursued to promote U.S. economic interests in ASEAN also have application to other areas, but can be particularly important to ASEAN. What American policy should be is related in part to what Japanese policy is being pursued. The obvious strategy to adopt is one that builds on U.S. economic strength and not weakness. The areas of comparative advantage for the United States consistent with an expanding U.S. standard of living are likely to be in temperate agricultural products, certain natural resource products like coal, the provision of various services, and the production (and servicing) of high-technology prod-

1. For a full discussion, see Robert O. Tilman, "Asia, ASEAN, and America in the Eighties: The Agonies of Maturing Relationships," *Contemporary Southeast Asia*, vol. 2 (March 1981), pp. 308–22.

2. *East Asia Study Mission, January 5–14, 1980*, report prepared for the use of the Joint Economic Committee, 96 Cong. 2 sess. (Government Printing Office, 1980).

ucts. The aim of policy should be to encourage American firms to provide such goods and services to foreign customers either directly or through foreign affiliates. For standardized products like wheat or coal in which international competition is centered on price and availability, the policy task is straightforward if not easily accomplished: namely, to enlarge market access and to obtain at least as favorable status as other non-ASEAN suppliers have.

Appropriate policy for the promotion of American services in ASEAN is more difficult to design because little is known about how the various service industries operate, how government policy affects them, and what the remedies are to problems that may exist. The U.S. government is beginning to gather the basic information, but it may be some time before policy analysis can be undertaken.

For high-technology products the tasks are more visible, though complex. The strongest barrier to successful penetration of a market is lack of knowledge. In general, it is difficult and expensive to obtain knowledge about developing countries, like the members of ASEAN, but the government can reduce the cost through what it does directly and what it encourages in the private sector. It can, for example, assist in the collection and transmission of knowledge through its own representatives in foreign countries. The recently created Foreign Commercial Service is a step in the right direction, but this organization must become a reality in the field, not just in Washington. The Japan External Trade Organization would be a good model to follow. Information should be collected on immediate market opportunities arising from new government contracts and industry transactions and also on medium-term prospects determined by government development plans and market trends.

Government policy can also aid in this process by encouraging efficient forms of information gathering in private industry. Instead, U.S. laws have been perverse in preventing the formation of broad-based general trading companies that include banks or other financial entities. ASEAN markets are well disposed toward trading company activities, the main organizational form used by the Japanese and one that is being emulated by Koreans, the Taiwanese, and others. Indeed, efforts are now being made in both the Philippines and Thailand to create general trading companies. The success of a general trading company depends on its ability to obtain market information and make maximum use of it. Therefore, it must be able to package so-called complete deals involving not only such things as design services, exports of machinery, managing construction, and technological training but also finance. Since U.S. antitrust laws now stand in the way of American trading companies of this sort, the Japanese and others have a significant advantage. Efforts already undertaken to change U.S. laws should be speedily completed.

After information is obtained by the government, it must be transmitted effectively to American industry. A good way to do this would be by forming industry committees within the Department of Commerce. The Japanese Ministry of International Trade and Industry provides a useful model. Each committee should be open to all American firms in the industry and be serviced by government employees knowledgeable about the industry. The more that is known about the capabilities of the particular American industry, the better can be the guidelines given government representatives in the field as to the type of information most beneficial to the industry in meeting foreign competition. Specialized missions to ASEAN countries jointly sponsored by government and industry would be a natural extension of the program.

Information gathering and transmission has been given primary importance because it is essential in competing for high-technology markets. At the same time, some new technology is also being created in ASEAN countries. The development of new ways to capture geothermal power in the Philippines is an example. American firms can keep abreast of such developments by being willing to form joint ventures in ASEAN countries. Of particular value would be American participation in ASEAN complementarity schemes (discussed in chapter 2). These involve the formation of industrial clubs to promote cooperation among different firms in the same industry within ASEAN for the purpose of achieving economies of scale through specialization. Foreign-owned firms will probably be permitted to participate, though possibly with some restrictions. Japanese firms will most likely participate if allowed to do so. American firms might be reluctant, however. It is possible to regard such clubs as a violation of U.S. antitrust laws, although any real threat to commerce in the United States is remote. It would be desirable to clarify the U.S. law so as to explicitly permit, and thereby encourage, American participation.

Continual criticism of the extraterritorial reach of U.S. laws is being expressed in many countries, and the United States must be responsive to it or suffer serious commercial damage. Indeed it is time to bring U.S. antitrust laws into the reality of the last quarter of the twentieth century. Competition is worldwide, and the world market must be considered the unit of operation. Ignoring the competition provided to large American firms by foreign firms of equal or larger size is both analytically wrong and commercially dangerous.

The United States must also be able to offer competitive financing terms and insurance for exports to and investment in ASEAN. This requires a vigorous program by both the Export-Import Bank and the Overseas Private Investment Corporation. The extension of export credits below market rates of interest is a form of export credit subsidy. It could be argued that any credit subsidy is unnecessary, or that some other form of subsidy would be more efficient. Such criticism is not valid. The credit subsidy is justified if it permits American firms to export by competing on equal terms with the Japanese. Exports provide externalities for the U.S. economy. And the form of the subsidy is determined by the importer; if credit terms are what the importer demands, it is an efficient subsidy. Perhaps an agreement with Japan and other industrial countries to limit credit subsidies is desirable— some progress has in fact been made in that direction—but obviously it requires multilateral negotiation.

Basically what is being suggested to meet Japanese competition in ASEAN and other areas is the establishment of a new relationship between the U.S. government and American business. Cooperation between government and business should replace the confrontation that has sometimes marked their relations. There is a proper role for the government in the private economy that need not and should not be intrusive. American firms must compete vigorously for export markets. The rules of the game and the modalities of behavior in these markets are not determined by the United States, but collectively by all countries. And in most countries government has a larger role in the economy than in the United States. Close cooperation between the U.S. government and industry will be required if the United States is to prosper in such an atmosphere. Certain commercial opportunities will arise within a government-to-government context, even though in the United States such matters are normally handled by the private sector. The U.S. government must be able to respond positively to such overtures or lose out to foreign competitors.

Gearing up for international competition need not and should not dictate the role of government within the U.S. economy. Nevertheless, the mistakes of U.S. domestic policy are sometimes seen more clearly in an international setting. Private capitalism works best at promoting efficient production in the United States when the government tries only to set fair rules for all business firms and provide a healthy macroeconomic environment. This does not include helping weak firms or industries at the expense of strong ones. To shore up a Chrysler at the expense of a Ford or a General Motors may make political sense domestically, but it is the wrong way to compete in world markets. Similarly, to protect a clothing industry at the expense of a larger computer industry means sacrificing high-paying for low-paying jobs, a measure that appears shortsighted in the extreme. If the government provides the proper atmosphere for the economy to grow and does not discriminate among firms and industries, it can cooperate with American businesses to promote their international competitiveness without overstepping its appropriate role in the economy. It is my belief that the market is the best regulator of economic behavior in the United States and that government interference is not justified unless market imperfections are present that can be corrected by government action.

Dealing with ASEAN as an Institution

As Robert Pringle has observed, there is a "need for a reorientation of our foreign policy process away from its traditional preoccupation with crisis, in order to deal more effectively with the 'low politics' issues of trade, technology, development, and environment which are now of primary importance in U.S. relations with most countries of the Third World."[3] "Low politics" is the preoccupation of American business. If a more cooperative relationship existed between business and government at home, American business could become an essential partner in the formation of appropriate U.S. foreign economic policy. American business could provide essential information about what is happening in the ASEAN economies, on what economic policy issues exist and are likely to arise, on what ASEAN governments want from the U.S. government, and on what, from the business perspective, should be the appropriate American response or initiative. The conduit for the business community to the government should probably be the Foreign Commercial Service, which would advise the secretary of commerce. Thus the secretary of commerce would have an enhanced role in formulating U.S. foreign economic policy.

Unlike the secretary of state, the secretary of commerce can avoid being caught up in crisis management. It should be the secretary of commerce's role to ensure that in foreign economic policy sufficient attention is given to

3. Robert Pringle, *Indonesia and the Philippines: American Interests in Island Southeast Asia* (Columbia University Press, 1980), p. x.

the "wheel that is not squeaking." The same sort of relationship should develop between the State and Commerce departments regarding economic policy as exists between State and Defense on security issues. Of course, the overall direction of foreign policy should remain with the secretary of state.

With respect to ASEAN, the United States should take the institution just as seriously as the member countries themselves do. An appropriate institutional response would be to create an ASEAN section within the Foreign Commercial Service. That section would take the responsibility for ensuring an appropriate U.S. policy stance. Also a deputy assistant secretary of state should be designated for ASEAN affairs under the assistant secretary of state for Asia and the Pacific. Such a person would be responsible for institutional developments, including the preparation of ASEAN-U.S. dialogues. When the time becomes appropriate, an American ambassador to ASEAN should be appointed.

The United States can also take substantive actions to demonstrate interest in ASEAN. It should urge the Asian Development Bank to increase lending programs that support integrative projects. The bank would then have to give greater attention to ASEAN's potential for economic development than it has in the past. The United States should be prepared to increase its funding of the bank for this purpose.

U.S. relations with ASEAN countries must not be only bilateral, however, and ignore the Asia-Pacific context of these countries. Indeed, much has been written about the desirability of creating a new institutional framework for relations among all the countries of the Pacific basin.[4] It is now generally agreed that such an institution would include both developed and developing countries; that it would provide for participation by academics, business people, and government officials in their private capacities; and that the frame of reference would encompass social, cultural, and economic affairs. Since participation by the ASEAN countries and the United States would be critical in its creation, the institution would provide a regional forum in which many U.S.-ASEAN issues could be fruitfully discussed and consultations held.

4. See Sir John Crawford, ed., *Pacific Economic Cooperation: Suggestions for Action* (Singapore: Heinemann Educational Books (Asia) Ltd, 1981); and *Pacific Region Interdependencies*, compendium of papers submitted to the Joint Economic Committee, 97 Cong. 1 sess. (GPO, 1981).

Eliminating Disincentives to Trade

Several elements of U.S. policy can be criticized for hampering American firms in their competitive struggle with Japanese and other firms: in particular, the Foreign Corrupt Practices Act, enacted in 1977; the human rights amendments (the so-called Harkin amendments) that were added to various U.S. laws during 1977–78; the taxation of Americans abroad as legislated in 1976 and amended in 1978; and the continued limitations of the Webb-Pomerene exemptions from antitrust law. U.S. policy should be changed to remove these disincentives to international trade.

The Foreign Corrupt Practices Act

This act makes it illegal for an American firm to try to influence a foreign official by means of money, offers, or gifts.[5] While seemingly unobjectionable on its face, the act in reality is a burden to American firms conducting legitimate business in ASEAN countries and is an irritant in U.S. relations with these countries.

One need not countenance corruption to believe that the whole approach was mistaken and that at a very minimum the act ought to be extensively revised. In order to force American business to treat corruption seriously and to prevent management from using ignorance as a defense, Congress wrote the law with a heavy hand, especially with respect to the definition of corrupt practices, the provisions for record-keeping, and the penalties for violation.

The law defines a corrupt practice as any attempt to influence through improper means a foreign official in his official capacity and makes such an act illegal. The provision covers all U.S. companies, their employees, directors, stockholders, and agents. Even the actions of a foreign corporation in which an American firm owns only a minority interest or an action of a foreign agent with an official of his own government could be considered illegal under U.S. law. Congress was aware that in many countries so-called grease payments are universally made to people operating in official capacities to obtain such things as permits and visas, which are almost impossible to obtain without such payments. Government employees in those countries are often miserably paid and accept the payments as part of their regular income. Congress tried to permit such facilitation payments by excluding from the designation "foreign official" any employee of a

5. Foreign Corrupt Practices Act of 1977 (91 Stat. 1494).

foreign government whose duties are essentially ministerial or clerical. However, since it is impossible to know how high the official is who shares in the payments, much uncertainty is involved.

The law also specifies that firms must keep records and institute accounting procedures that make it possible to trace transactions and the disposition of assets in "reasonable detail," to ensure that all transactions are "executed with management's general or specific authorization." This provision goes far beyond the usual requirements for accounting detail, which include only items considered material to the company's financial statements.

Violations could result in fines of $1 million for the firm and fines of $10,000 or five years in jail, or both, for individuals, but the individual must be a U.S. citizen, national, or resident to be subject to U.S. jurisdiction. Enforcement powers were given to both the Justice Department and the Securities and Exchange Commission. Thus a chief executive officer of an American firm could conceivably be sent to jail for five years for an action by a foreign agent of the firm in a foreign country, even though that action was perfectly acceptable under the customs of that country and was authorized only by presumption. While this example is rather farfetched, such illegal acts no doubt take place continually. It is easy to understand why many executive officers do not find it desirable to try to export their goods and services.

There are three basic problems with the law: it imposes on all U.S. firms a significant cost of compliance, which must be passed along in higher prices; it creates tremendous uncertainty for U.S. firms about whether they are violating the law or not; and it ensures a loss of export business for U.S. firms because foreign firms are not similarly constrained and are thus led to compete by "illegal" methods. It is for the latter reason that some observers believe the law has actually encouraged corruption.[6] Furthermore, some foreign governments and observers resent the intrusion of U.S. law into their countries. Most, if not all, ASEAN countries have their own laws against what they consider to be corruption and enforce them as they see fit. They have not sought U.S. assistance in enforcing their laws and resent the implication that corruption is a serious problem only in their countries and not in the United States and that they are incapable of handling it.

As discussed in chapter 4, some indirect evidence suggests that U.S. exports of high-technology products to Indonesia and the Philippines have

6. *East Asia Study Mission.*

been hurt by the Foreign Corrupt Practices Act. In a survey conducted by the General Accounting Office, 30 percent of the largest American exporters perceived a loss of export business because of the act.[7] Also, some firms have even closed offices and withdrawn from doing business in Indonesia and the Philippines. Apparently, while many Americans can do business in these countries without violating U.S. laws, others cannot.

Some revision of the act is already being considered through amendments introduced by Senator John H. Chafee (Republican of Rhode Island).[8] At a minimum, revisions should clarify the meaning of a corrupt practice and confine it to actions that reasonable local people consider illegal, reduce the accounting burden of staying in compliance, and simplify enforcement procedures. First, Americans should not be put into legal jeopardy by U.S. law because of transactions between foreigners unless evidence exists that Americans have commissioned a crime. Second, it should not be considered illegal for Americans to conform with local law and custom. Thus small gifts and payments should be excluded from the law unless they exceeded normal practice. Third, accounting responsibility should be limited to generally accepted accounting principles. Clearly, falsification and attempts to circumvent the law cannot be acceptable. Finally, enforcement of the act should be limited to the Justice Department. These changes would remove the disincentives faced by honest Americans who want to export.

Human Rights Amendments

During the 1970s human rights amendments were added to U.S. legislation authorizing economic and security assistance, to authorizations of loans by the Export-Import Bank, and insurance issued by the Overseas Private Investment Corporation. It is unlikely that these amendments have had severe consequences for U.S. exports to ASEAN countries, though they added some uncertainty to export transactions involving Export-Import Bank loans, which could be disallowed at the last minute.

No doubt the policy of upholding human rights is based on moral principles strongly felt in the United States. Since it is a fundamental part of U.S. society, it is necessarily part of U.S. foreign policy. Furthermore, it is

7. General Accounting Office, *Impact of the Foreign Corrupt Practices Act on U.S. Business*, report to the Congress of the United States by the Comptroller General (GAO, 1981).

8. Business Accounting and Foreign Trade Simplification Bill (S.B. 708), 97 Cong. 2 sess.

desirable and useful to differentiate the United States from the Soviet Union and other totalitarian states where, as a matter of ideology, elemental individual rights are subordinated to the needs of the state. Nevertheless, questions of the appropriateness of human rights criteria can be raised, especially concerning the use of leverage arising from unrelated actions for this purpose.

The strongest message the United States can transmit to other countries comes from the practice of human rights in the United States and the example it sets. However, what the United States says and proclaims as its policy is also important; rhetoric and symbols do matter in foreign policy. And certainly the United States clearly must avoid direct participation in the violation of human rights in other countries. The case for going beyond this point, however, becomes murky and may not be well founded.

Contrary to what some would say, U.S. contacts with foreign governments do not imply U.S. approval of their human rights policies, nor can U.S. actions determine these policies. Selling wheat to the Russians, for example, does not imply that the United States approves of the limitations that the Soviet Union places on emigration by its citizens, nor would denying such sales encourage it to modify that policy. Furthermore, it is not in the interest of the United States to politicize commercial transactions and make a mockery of market mechanisms. Since both sides gain from a commercial transaction, interrupting it hurts both of them. Therefore, a country should always exercise great care in placing barriers to international commerce, because they hurt the country itself and because they seldom if ever achieve their intended purpose.

Taxation of Americans Abroad

Two competing and incompatible concepts of tax equity are involved in the taxing of citizens of one country who work in another. One theory states that citizens working abroad should be taxed no differently from citizens working at home. Thus, for example, if the tax on earnings levied by Japan is less than that levied by the United States, the U.S. government should claim for itself the difference between the two levies on earnings of Americans working in Japan. The other theory says that the person working in a foreign country should be taxed no differently from the citizens of that country with whom he must compete. Thus, for example, a Japanese working in the Philippines should be liable for taxes to the Philippines but not to Japan. Appealing arguments can be made for both theories. The United

States applies the first theory, but all other major countries use the second. Some Americans believed that if the United States showed the way in taxing foreign income, others would follow, but that expectation has been disappointed.

In 1926 the U.S. tax code recognized that working abroad entails special costs and problems for Americans and granted a special exclusion from taxable income to reflect those costs.[9] But in 1976 Congress became convinced that the exclusion was too generous and along with two tax court rulings significantly raised the effective tax burden.[10] Because of strong objections, enforcement of the provisions of the 1976 law were delayed in 1977 and partly replaced by a new law in 1978.[11] Furthermore, as part of the comprehensive tax reduction legislated in 1981, various provisions of the 1978 act were liberalized, which greatly reduced the tax burden on Americans working abroad. The question remaining is whether the United States should emulate the practice of other countries and not attempt to tax foreign income at all.

Given the government's need for revenue, the presumption must be on the side of sustaining rather than narrowing the tax base. However, there are good arguments on the other side. If Americans are taxed more heavily than other nationals when they work abroad, it is more expensive for firms to hire Americans; therefore, firms try to minimize their use and replace them with foreigners whenever possible. This is likely to reduce U.S. exports. American designers working in construction abroad, for example, usually specify U.S. equipment with which they are familiar. Econometric evidence suggests that a positive relation exists between the number of Americans working abroad and U.S. exports: a 10 percent reduction in Americans would lead to a 5 percent reduction in U.S. exports.[12] The effect would probably be greatest in developing countries such as the ASEAN ones.

Because of the changes made in the tax law in 1981,[13] the issue may no longer be important from a practical point of view, but the question remains whether the United States can continue to handicap American busi-

9. Section 911 of the Internal Revenue Code. Sections 119 and 913 also have a bearing on an individual's tax burden.

10. Tax Reform Act of 1976 (90 Stat. 1520); and tax court cases: Philip H. Stephens, T. C. Memo 1976-13, and James H. McDonald, 66 TC 223 (1976).

11. Foreign Earned Income Act of 1978 (94 Stat. 194).

12. John Mutti, *The American Presence Abroad and U.S. Exports*, U.S. Treasury Department, Office of Tax Analysis Paper 33 (OTA, 1978).

13. Economic Recovery Tax Act of 1981, P.L. 97-34.

ness in its competitive struggle against the Japanese and others in ASEAN countries and elsewhere without suffering a significant societal loss. Given the importance of meeting the Japanese challenge, such handicaps should be minimized.

Antitrust Laws

The clear purpose of U.S. antitrust laws is to safeguard competition within the U.S. economy. When applied to international commerce, however, U.S. laws, as currently drawn, often act to reduce U.S. competitiveness. The laws were intended to apply to both the domestic and foreign commerce of American companies, to foreign firms doing business in the United States, and to the activity of American firms abroad. The extraterritorial application of these laws has annoyed many countries and has resulted in juridical conflict with some, including Australia, Canada, and the United Kingdom.

Congress recognized that the antitrust laws could be too restrictive toward U.S. exports, and consequently authorized modifications through the Webb-Pomerene Act of 1918, which allows American firms to cooperate for export purposes. However, the law has not been very effective.[14] In 1979 there were only thirty-three Webb-Pomerene associations, which accounted for only 2 percent of U.S. exports and were apparently successful only in the export of motion picture and television film and standardized raw materials.[15]

The Webb-Pomerene Act has several defects. First, it covers goods but not services. Second, it confines permitted activity to the act of exporting and thereby eliminates other activities that may be necessary in order to export. Finally, it leaves business firms unsure whether they can be prosecuted under other antitrust laws for restraining trade in the United States when they combine for export purposes.

One way to make American firms more competitive would be to amend the Webb-Pomerene Act itself. Provisions could be written to take care of its deficiencies as well as to permit American firms to enter ASEAN industry clubs. A better approach would be to authorize export trading compa-

14. 40 Stat. 516.
15. See testimony of Luther H. Hodges, former under secretary of commerce, and C. Fred Bergsten, former assistant secretary of the treasury for international affairs, in *Export Trading Companies and Trade Association*, Hearings before the Subcommittee on International Finance of the Committee on Banking, Housing, and Urban Affairs, 96 Cong. 1 sess. (GPO, 1979), pp. 2–40.

nies, as discussed earlier. U.S. legislative efforts have already begun to authorize such companies, and they offer a more comprehensive solution to the antitrust law problem. While seemingly an unimportant matter, trading companies are of significance for U.S. trading success in ASEAN countries and worthy of high legislative priority.

Summary

In all the problems just reviewed, the United States recognized a certain difficulty and took unilateral legislative and executive action to deal with it. Because the problems are international in scope, the U.S. approach could at best provide only an indirect and partial solution and at worst exacerbate the problem, as with corrupt practices. In every instance American firms were handicapped relative to their competitors, and U.S. exports suffered. International problems require multinational solutions, that is, agreements and understanding among countries that grow out of a process of international discussion and negotiation. The United States must try to convince others that a particular problem requires attention. If it cannot, action should be delayed until the case can be made. Indeed, it is possible for the United States to be wrong in its assessment. However, if international understanding and agreement can be reached, the problem will be dealt with correctly and without penalizing American business. Unfortunately many past unilateral U.S. actions may stand in the way of international agreement, since other countries will not want to give up the competitiveness advantage that those actions have given them.

Encouraging U.S. Imports of ASEAN Products

As noted in chapter 4, U.S. imports of merchandise from ASEAN countries rose 26.8 percent a year during the 1970s, a higher rate of growth than total U.S. imports; thus ASEAN countries increased their shares of the U.S. market. Furthermore, more U.S. imports from ASEAN were manufactured goods, particularly finished rather than semifinished manufactures. Because ASEAN firms have had little success in exporting finished manufactures to the more closed Japanese market, the United States has gained considerable goodwill in ASEAN countries. They would prefer to buy U.S. products than Japanese ones if they are equally competitive.

The United States could do even more to welcome imports from

ASEAN countries to enhance this goodwill. While strong measures like preferential tariff reductions would be inappropriate, other measures that would not be overtly discriminatory are possible. They include encouragement of trade missions from ASEAN countries, favorable bilateral treatment under the multifiber agreement for textiles, improvement of the general system of tariff preference for products of special interest to ASEAN countries, and a willingness to discuss trade issues with the ASEAN countries if difficulties should arise. For example, the United States should be able to work out a cooperative effort with ASEAN producers so that tin sales from the U.S. stockpile would not disrupt the market. Similar measures could conceivably be added to the list after discussion with U.S. and ASEAN business people. It is important that the United States continue to be a major importer of ASEAN products, since all the countries involved will benefit.

Conclusion

The focus of this study has been the economic relations between the United States and the ASEAN countries with an eye to meeting the Japanese economic challenge. Increasing exports and investment are essential to the economic well-being of the United States, and ASEAN countries can make a significant contribution to this goal. These countries represent the growing markets in the world in which American business must do well if the American economy is going to prosper. Doing well in ASEAN markets will require American firms to meet Japanese competition successfully under conditions in which neither has an artificial advantage.

The foundation for competitive success of American firms in ASEAN countries will be laid in the United States. If the American economy manages to sustain reasonably strong and noninflationary growth, then American firms can be competitive abroad. Improving the economic performance of the American economy requires not only better macroeconomic policy by the government, but also the creation of a more cooperative relationship between the government and business. Similarly, industrial relations within the United States must turn away from confrontation and move toward cooperation. With enlightened management, American labor can be led to understand that job security and real wage gain depend on the noninflationary growth of the economy.

Even more can be done to improve American competitiveness in

ASEAN markets. Those American laws that discourage exports to and foreign investment in ASEAN countries can be revised. The Foreign Corrupt Practices Act, the human rights amendments, the taxation of Americans abroad, and the antitrust laws can be changed to reflect the realities of the world marketplace.

The time has come for the United States to make a commitment to creating an outward-looking economy. In the past a diversified resource base, a large and varied labor force, and a continental-size country made inward-focused economic development a possible and not very expensive economic strategy for the United States. That is no longer the case. The United States has much to contribute to other countries. It also has much to gain by intense interaction with the world economy. The United States should therefore gear its policy toward maximizing the gains from economic interdependence, which will be essential for America's prosperity in the 1980s and beyond.

Commodity Classification System

International trade in commodities is classified by the United Nations into ten broad groups, labeled by the one-digit numbers 0 to 9 (standard international trade classification, or SITC). These categories, when finally disaggregated, number approximately 1,300 basic items, each of which is identified by a four-digit—or in some cases, a five-digit—code. These basic items, when summed, compose total commodity trade for a given reporting country and partner country.[1]

To create a manageable data bank, the UN trade data were initially aggregated into 106 commodity groups, which taken together represent total trade. For the purposes of this study, the category "goods, not elsewhere specified" (SITC 9 less 951) was then excluded because it is composed of goods without any common traits.

In order to test the Heckscher-Ohlin theorem for U.S.-ASEAN and Japanese-ASEAN trade, the 105 commodities were classified into four groups according to their relative factor intensities. These groups are natural resource–intensive, unskilled labor–intensive, technology-intensive, and human capital–intensive goods (table A-1).

The commodity classification procedure was performed sequentially by initially categorizing the commodities whose factor intensities are most apparent. First, the natural resource–based goods were identified. This group consists of all commodities within SITC section 0–4 (that is, food and live animals, beverages and tobacco, crude materials, mineral fuels, and animal and vegetable oils), and SITC classes 61 (leather), 63 (plywood), 68 (nonferrous metals), 661–63 (mineral manufactures), and 667 (diamonds). There were forty-two commodities in this group.

Second, by using the groupings of commodities according to their respective value added per worker, as presented by Garnaut and

---

1. A detailed listing of the classification system used in this study is presented in the United Nations, *Standard International Trade Classification, Revised*, series M, no. 34 (New York: UN Statistical Office, 1961).

Table A-1. *SITC Designations for Products in International Trade*

Commodity	SITC, revised	Commodity	SITC, revised
Natural resource intensive		Nonferrous	
Meat	00, 01	manufactures	6832, 6852, 6862,
Dairy	02		6872, 688, 689
Fish	03	Unwrought aluminum	6841
Wheat	041	Aluminum	
Rice	042	manufactures	6842
Other cereals	043, 045–47		
Corn	046	*Unskilled labor intensive*	
Prepared foods	048, 0713, 09	Yarn	651
Fruit	051–53	Fabrics	652, 653
Vegetables	054, 055	Textile products	654–57
Sugar	06	Glass	664–66
Coffee	0711, 0712	Ships	7353, 7358, 7359
Cacao	072–75	Firearms	7351, 951
Feed	08	Furniture	82
Beverages	11	Clothing	82
Tobacco	12	Footwear	85
Hides	21	Miscellaneous	
Soybeans	22	consumer products	81, 83, 893, 895,
Crude rubber	23		899
Wood	24	Toys	894
Pulp	25		
Cotton	263	*Technology intensive*	
Fibers	261, 262, 264–69	Chemical elements	51
Iron ore	281, 282	Medicine	54
Nonferrous ore	283–86	Fertilizer	56
Crude materials, not		Plastics	58
elsewhere specified	29	Other chemicals	52, 57, 59
Coal	32	Power generating	
Gas, natural and		equipment[a]	7111–13,
manufactured, and			7116–18
electric current	34, 35	Jet engines[a]	7114
Crude petroleum	331	Car engines[a]	7115
Petroleum products	332	Tractors	7125
Animal and vegetable		Agricultural machinery	7121–23, 7129
oils	4	Office machinery[a]	7141, 7149
Leather	61	Computers[a]	7142, 7143
Plywood	63	Metal working	
Mineral manufactures	661–63	machinery[a]	715
Diamonds	667	Textile machinery[a]	717
Pig iron	671	Mining machinery[a]	7184
Unwrought nonferrous		Other industrial	
metals	681, 6831, 6851,	machinery[a]	718, 7194–98
	6861, 6871	Heating and cooling	
Unwrought copper	6821	equipment[a]	7191
Copper manufactures	6822	Pumps[a]	7192
		Fork lifts	7193

Table A-1 (*continued*)

Commodity	SITC, revised	Commodity	SITC, revised
Electric power		Rubber	62
machinery[a]	722	Paper	64
Telecommunications		Steel	672–79
equipment[a]	7249	Metal manufacturing	691–94, 698
Electrical apparatus for		Cutlery	696, 697
medical purposes[a]	726	Hand tools	695
Transistors	7293	Machine parts	7199
Electrical measuring		Televisions	7241
equipment[a]	7295	Radios	7242
Electrical apparatus[a]	723, 7291, 7292,	Domestic electrical	
	7296, 7297,	apparatus	725
	7299	Trains	731
Scientific equipment[a]	8617–19	Cars	7321
Optical equipment[a]	8611–13	Trucks	7322–25
Aircraft[a]	734	Road motor vehicle	
Cameras	8614–16	parts	7236–28, 7294
Film	862, 863	Motorcycles	7329
		Trailers	733
		Watches	864
Human capital intensive		Phonographs	891
Paints	53	Books	892
Perfumes	55	Jewelry	896, 897

Source: SITC numbers from United Nations, *Standard International Classification, Revised*, series M, no. 34 (New York: UN Statistical Office, 1961). This classification scheme was in effect from 1960 to 1975.

a. Non-price-sensitive technology-intensive products. The other technology-intensive products listed are price sensitive.

Anderson,[2] eleven goods were classified as unskilled labor intensive. These commodities, representing those with the lowest value added per worker, are the same goods appearing in Garnaut and Anderson, except where the commodity aggregations precluded separating goods further. Included in this group are such SITC classes as 65 (textiles and fabrics), 664–66 (glass), 735 (ships and boats), 81–85, 893–95, 899 (miscellaneous consumer goods, furniture, clothing, footwear, and toys), and 951 (firearms).

The remaining commodities were divided into technology-intensive and human capital–intensive categories by selecting as technology intensive those goods with the highest ratios of research and development expendi-

2. Ross Garnaut and Kym Anderson, "ASEAN Export Specialisation and the Evolution of Comparative Advantage in the Western Pacific Region," in Ross Garnaut, ed., *ASEAN in a Changing Pacific and World Economy* (Miami: Australian National University Press, 1980), p. 411. The presentation in Garnaut and Anderson is based on work in Bela Balassa, "A 'Stages Approach' to Comparative Advantage," World Bank Staff Working Paper 256 (May 1977), appendix table 1.

tures to value added.[3] Ratios were calculated by industry, classified according to two- and three-digit standard industrial classifications (SIC), for the average of the years 1967–68 and 1975–76. The SIC classes were then cross-classified by using Balassa's system correlating SIC and SITC.[4] There are thirty commodities in the technology-intensive category, including SITC divisions 51 (chemical elements), 54 (medicine), 56 (fertilizer), 58 (plastics), 52, 57, 59 (other chemicals), 71 less 7199 (machinery), 7249 (telecommunications equipment), 726 (electric apparatus for medical purposes), 7293 (transistors), 7295 (electrical measuring apparatus), 723, 7291, 7292, 7296–99 (electrical apparatus, not elsewhere specified), 734 (aircraft), 861 (scientific, medical, and optical measuring apparatus), and 862–63 (photographic supplies).

Human capital–intensive goods are those that have relatively lower research and development expenditures to value-added ratios than do technology-intensive goods. Among the twenty-two commodities falling under the human capital–intensive rubric are SITC groups 53 (paints), 55 (perfumes), 62 (rubber), 64 (paper), 672–79 (steel), 69 (manufactures of metal, not elsewhere specified), 7199 (machine parts), 7241 (televisions), 7242 (radios), 725 (domestic electrical apparatus), 7294 (automotive electrical equipment), 735 (trains), 732 (trailers), 864 (watches), 891 (phonographs), 892 (books), and 896–97 (jewelry).

After it was found that the United States appears to have a comparative advantage in the production of technology-intensive goods, these commodities were further separated into two subgroups: price sensitive and non price sensitive. This division involved decisions based on a priori judgments about the nature of the products considered. As seen in the table, eleven commodities were judged to be price sensitive, and nineteen were judged to be non price sensitive.

3. Research and development figures were taken from National Science Foundation, *Research and Development in Industry*, 1978 (National Science Foundation, 1980); value added were from Bureau of the Census, *Annual Survey of Manufactures*.

4. See appendix table 2 in Balassa, " 'Stages' Approach to Comparative Advantage."

Index